S. Hrg. 113–394

# RESOURCES AS REVENUE

# HEARING

BEFORE THE

## COMMITTEE ON
## ENERGY AND NATURAL RESOURCES
## UNITED STATES SENATE

ONE HUNDRED THIRTEENTH CONGRESS

SECOND SESSION

TO

FOCUS ON THE STATE AND LOCAL GOVERNMENT BENEFITS IN TERMS OF REVENUE GENERATION AND JOBS CREATED FROM NATURAL RE-SOURCE PRODUCTION

JULY 22, 2014

Printed for the use of the
Committee on Energy and Natural Resources

U.S. GOVERNMENT PRINTING OFFICE

89–711 PDF          WASHINGTON : 2014

For sale by the Superintendent of Documents, U.S. Government Printing Office
Internet: bookstore.gpo.gov   Phone: toll free (866) 512–1800; DC area (202) 512–1800
Fax: (202) 512–2104   Mail: Stop IDCC, Washington, DC 20402–0001

(II)

# CONTENTS

## STATEMENTS

Page

Gould, Gregory, Director, Office of Natural Resource Revenue, Department of the Interior .................................................................................................... 6
Landrieu, Hon. Mary L., U.S. Senator From Louisiana ..................................... 1
Murkowski, Hon. Lisa, U.S. Senator From Alaska .............................................. 3
Nelson, Laura, Director of the Utah Governor's Office of Energy Development, Salt Lake City, UT ............................................................................................ 25
Pearce, Paul, President, National Forest Counties and Schools Coalition, STE-VENSON, WA ..................................................................................................... 18
Randolph, Charlotte A., President, Lafourche Parish, Thibodaux, LO .............. 14
Shafer, Sean, Consulting Manager, Quest Offshore Resources, Inc., Sugar Land, TX ............................................................................................................. 22
Taylor, Duane, Director, Federal Affairs, Motorcycle Industry Council, Arlington, VA .................................................................................................................. 31
Webster, Joel, Director, Center for Western Lands, Theodore Roosevelt Conservation Partnership, Missoula, MT ................................................................ 19

## APPENDIXES

### APPENDIX I

Responses to additional questions ........................................................................ 47

### APPENDIX II

Additional material submitted for the record ....................................................... 51

# RESOURCES AS REVENUE

## TUESDAY, JULY 22, 2014

U.S. SENATE,
COMMITTEE ON ENERGY AND NATURAL RESOURCES,
*Washington, DC.*

The committee met, pursuant to notice, at 10:36 a.m. in room SD–366, Dirksen Senate Office Building, Hon. Mary L. Landrieu, chair, presiding.

### OPENING STATEMENT OF HON. MARY L. LANDRIEU, U.S. SENATOR FROM LOUISIANA

The CHAIR. Good morning. Welcome to our Energy and Natural Resource Committee meeting this morning, Leveraging America's Resources and Revenue Generator and Job Creator.

Thank all of our members for attending. We're going to have a busy morning. I think a very informative panel.

We thank you, Director Gould, for being with us this morning.

We are going to have votes called at 10:45, a series of 3. So we hope to get through this panel. We'll leave at the end of the vote time and then recess for a half an hour and then come back for the second panel.

I thank all of you for being with us this morning to consider the production and distribution of the value of America's natural resources. We have a short list including oil, gas, coal, minerals, including gold, copper, lead, zinc, uranium. We have grazing and timber. Our revenues, recreational fees that range from entrance fees to our beautiful parks, cabin rentals, for example, boat launch rentals and others. So this is a very short list, but gives a sense of what our Committee is going to be exploring.

How these revenues are generated?

How they are shared?

How we can be better stewards?

We will explore just how much revenue is generated from all sources and how this revenue is distributed.

We will also explore and expand and improve our revenue sharing partnerships with States and communities that share the responsibilities, both advantages and disadvantages of this production.

To enhance our stewardship of these natural resources.

This is an issue that Senator Murkowski and I have cared a great deal about for a long period of time coming from very rich, natural resource States. I'm pleased that she has joined me in this oversight effort.

Since 1985 America's natural resources have generated $248 billion of revenue for our Treasury, an average of about $9 billion a year. I am extremely interested in hearing from our witnesses about how we can ensure these revenues, have been part of our past, how we can ensure they'll be part of our future. How we can use them to continue to generate wealth, prosperity and jobs for the communities that are our partners in this production.

As many of you know I've been a long time advocate of full funding for the Land and Water Conservation Fund that was authorized and created in 1965. But only in two of the last 50 years has it ever been fully funded, as I'm sure was the vision of its creators. I think this is a challenge. I hope our Committee is up to meeting it.

Natural resource production has played a critical role for many States, Louisiana and Alaska, just to listing two. In the late 19 and early 20th century, newly formed western States faced the challenge of building adequate infrastructure to support their rapidly expanding populations and economic development. At the same time many of these States, especially Wyoming and New Mexico, discovered abundant reserves of critical natural resources such as oil, gas, coal and other minerals.

Under the 1872 Minerals Leasing Act individuals and private investors had free reign to harness these natural resources on Federal lands and could claim private ownership of any minerals they discovered. States were then able to use property taxes and other revenues from these lands to finance their budgets, provide basic services to their growing population.

However, over time these laws changed. The oil boom of the early 20th century prompted the Federal Government to reassess its Minerals Lands Use policy so that not only private interests were served, but public interest could be served as well. Congress stepped in and passed the Minerals Land Act of 1920 which provided the foundation of revenue sharing partnership that some States enjoy to this day.

Then, as offshore oil and natural gas production continued to grow in the years following World War II, Congress passed the Outer Continental Shelf Lands Act of 1953 which claims submerged lands up to 200 miles around our coast. That act, one act in itself, expanded the territory of the United States by 10 percent.

Unfortunately that law, in my view, failed to expand revenue sharing to coastal States that hosted this new and lucrative offshore energy production. I'd like to correct that injustice. Have been working on it for more than 20 years and have made some significant progress passing GOMESA. But there's more work to be done.

In 2006 I was joined by Senator Pete Dominici, former Chair of this Committee. Together we passed GOMESA, the first law of its kind to establish and expand revenue sharing for the 4 energy producing Gulf States, Louisiana, Alabama, Mississippi and Texas. These States now share 37.5 percent of the revenues they produce. However, there was an arbitrary collective cap on these States placed at $500 million a year. No other State or group of States in the country operates under such a cap.

As our country continues to produce more energy offshore, GOMESA provides us a strong foundation to establish a more full partnership with all of our coastal States including Alaska. Our next step is to lift the cap to accelerate these payments and to make this more in line with interior States.

I have a bill before the Committee. There are others pending as well. The FAIR Act which has been introduced by Senator Murkowski, myself, Senator Begich along with the support of Senator Wyden, is a comprehensive approach to modifying the terms of this partnership to be more productive, I think, for the States and the country.

Louisiana is a very important part of our natural resource production. Other coastal States are as well. But the interior States produce a tremendous amount of energy for our country. Timber harvest on the lands are important. As I said, grazing rights, recreational revenues come in from both coastal and interior States.

In our second panel we will hear from Charlotte Randolph, the President of Lafourche Parish. She can speak to the specifics of the absence of more robust revenue sharing and what it's doing to her parish.

In conclusion, America's natural resources play a critical role in the economy of the United States, both a revenue generator and job creator. I'm looking forward to the testimony from our witnesses, both at the local level to see how it also affects local communities from coastal States to interior States.

I'd like to now turn to my Ranking Member, Senator Murkowski, for her opening statement. Thank her for her interest, her passion and her support to try to get this right for all 50 States, Senator. To really honor the work of our local communities in and recognize their partnership in production.

## STATEMENT OF HON. LISA MURKOWSKI, U.S. SENATOR FROM ALASKA

Senator MURKOWSKI. Thank you, Madame Chairman. Appreciate the work with you on these important issues.

I want to thank our witnesses, the Director, this morning and those that will be part of the second panel.

I really have one take home message this morning. It is as follows. The only way that American resources will generate revenue and create jobs is if American workers and businesses are allowed to access those resources. You have to have access.

Back in June the EIA released a report showing what's happened on Federal and Indian lands over the last 10 fiscal years.

We've seen coal production down 8 percent.

Crude oil and lease condensate production are down 11 percent.

Natural gas production is down 43 percent.

Overall, fossil fuel production from Federal and Indian lands declined, declined, by 21 percent over the past decade.

When we're talking about generating revenue and creating jobs we're really talking about increasing production. When we're talking about increasing production we're really talking about increasing access. So let's talk about access.

I know that people like to point out that most shale resources appear to be on State and private lands. That's why production from

State and private lands is so high right now. But that's not the case with our conventional resources.

Consider it the Arctic Coastal Plain within the non-wilderness portion of ANWR. According to USGS there are between 5.7 billion and 16 billion barrels of oil located there. If you take the mean estimate at 10.3 billion at a price of $100 per barrel and the taxes and royalties generated from that production would amount to some $153 billion over 30 years, $153 billion over 30 years.

That's not my math. That's coming from the Congressional Research Service, from CRS.

Consider the Alaska offshore region where the Bureau of Ocean Energy Management estimates contains some 26 billion barrels of oil and condensate plus another 132 trillion, with a T, cubic feet of natural gas.

Now every American has heard of the Gulf of Mexico and many have now heard of the Bakken and the Eagle Ford. I live and breathe for the day when every American will have also heard of the Chukchi, of the Beaufort, of Cook Inlet and other resource rich areas that we have in Alaska.

Now some accuse me of talking about Alaska too much. They say that the boom is really in the lower 48 right now. That Alaska has, kind of, missed out. Missed out on those revenues, missed out on those jobs.

But look at what's going on around the world.

We have Iraq ablaze.

Syria in turmoil.

Russia and Ukraine in Europe on the brink.

With energy security on everybody's mind and with policymakers here in Washington debating how, not whether, to use our energy resources as an instrument of national advantage, my answer is why not talk about Alaska? Why not talk about what we have up North?

Resources, of course, are more than just energy. Certainly the mining industry provides thousands and thousands of good jobs across the country as it provides the building blocks for nearly every other part of our economy. The Federal Government also made a promise over a century ago to actively manage our national forests and pay 25 percent of the receipts to counties, parishes and boroughs containing national forest land.

It was only fair because the Federal Government doesn't pay local taxes. So it would share revenue generated from these forests to help fund essential services such as schools and roads. These payments are often called National Forest Receipts or 25 percent payments.

Back in 1937 BLM also began sharing commercial receipts generated on Oregon and California grant railroad lands.

The primary source of commercial receipts for these revenue sharing programs is timber receipts. I can tell you for a while we cut a lot of timber and generated a fair amount of money. It created some good jobs, some very good jobs, in our rural communities that you could raise a family on. At the peak in 1989 the Forest Service shared approximately $362 million with counties and BLM O and C payments totaled about $110 million.

But all that changed, somewhat abruptly. Receipts generated have declined dramatically since. You only need to look at where we are today.

In Fiscal Year 2013 if revenue sharing had been used to make payments rather than Secure Rural Schools, the estimated 25 percent payment would have been just $58 million, the lower dotted line on there. That's $58 million for the entire forest.

In my home State of Alaska on the Tongass the devastation could not have been more apparent. Back in 1990 the Tongass supported a vibrant timber industry with more than one thousand good, middle income jobs. We harvested more than 400 million board feet and generated more than $47 million which we shared with communities across Southeast Alaska.

But do you know how much we're earning nowadays?

In FY2013 we barely harvested 35 million board feet. The receipts generated from that paltry harvest were just about a million dollars. That's a rounding error compared to where we used to be.

Those good jobs? We now have a third of the jobs, roughly 300 than we counted on in the 1990s.

So what happened?

What happened is that Federal, environmental policy, regulations, the 2001 Clinton Roadless Rule, the listing of the Northern Spotted Owl and the ensuing litigation halted timber harvesting on our national forests, crippled the timber industry. It turned many of our forests into tinderboxes and devastated the economies of rural communities across the West.

These days we actually burn more timber than we cut. We pay counties Secure Rural Schools money to basically look the other way. This is a travesty, Madame Chairman.

We've taken away the economic ability of these communities to survive on their own and make them dependent on Federal assistance. It's not the community's fault. Which is why I've supported the Secure Rural Schools extension and re-authorizations, but the status quo isn't sustainable either.

SRS was never meant to be a permanent entitlement. It was supposed to be a temporary safety net. So it's time we returned to actively managing our national forests and put our timber communities back to work.

Often we hear that we need to look at recreation and tourism as the economic engine of the future. We all recognize that these activities are important and no State, certainly, is more proud of our recreation activities than Alaska. But recreation and tourism are not adequate substitutes for responsible resource development on Federal lands.

In Alaska, for more than 50 years, we've shown that resource development, recreation and tourism can co-exist. We need to actively manage our Federal lands for multiple uses. If not, we should divest the Federal Government of those lands and let the States or the counties manage them.

Now some will paint this as a clear choice that is somewhat extreme. But we do need to address, head on, the fact that federally owned land has a profound impact on the communities that depend on them for their survival. I think we'll probably hear that from the witnesses in the second panel.

Thank you, Madame Chairman.

The CHAIR. Thank you for that excellent and very strong statement. You can see that I've got a passionate ranking member and partner here. I'm really looking forward to working with her as we move forward with a policy that is, I think, better for our local communities as job generators and for the public.

Director Gould, we'll take your opening statement. Then as earlier indicated we're going to take a break and come back for our questioning and our next panel.

## STATEMENT OF GREGORY GOULD, DIRECTOR, OFFICE OF NATURAL RESOURCE REVENUE, DEPARTMENT OF THE INTERIOR

Mr. GOULD. Madame Chair Landrieu, Ranking Member Murkowski and members of the committee, I appreciate the opportunity to be here today to talk about the State and local government benefits of revenue generated and jobs created from our Nation's natural resource production.

My name is Greg Gould. I'm the Director of the Office of Natural Resource Revenue or ONRR as we are called in the Department of Interior.

In 2011—in 2010 ONRR was established within the Office of the Secretary as part of a departmental reorganization. The reorganization presented an opportunity for the office to improve the management and oversight of the royalty and revenue collection and disbursement activities for the Department. ONRR is responsible for collecting, disbursing, verifying Federal and American Indian, natural resource revenues on behalf of all Americans.

At the Department of Interior we manage public lands and Federal waters. It is from these areas that we get the natural resources that are critical to our Nation's energy security. The lands and resources that the Department manages are vast.

For onshore lands there are Federal leases located in 34 States totaling more than 37 million acres.

Offshore, the Department has made 60 million acres available for development in just the past three offshore lease sales. In the Gulf of Mexico alone, there are over 32 million acres under active lease.

According to the Department's 2013 economic contributions report, Interior's activities contributed $360 billion to the U.S. economy supporting 2 million jobs and activities including outdoor recreation and tourism, energy development, grazing and timber harvest. In Fiscal Year 2013 ONRR disbursed more than $14 billion to the U.S. Treasury, various State and Indian accounts and special use accounts such as the Land and Water Conservation Fund. Included in that $14 billion, was $932 million disbursed to American Indian tribes and individual Indian mineral owners.

In 1982 with the passage of the Federal Oil and Gas Royalty Management Act the Department created a comprehensive, consolidated system for the collection, accounting and disbursement of these revenues. From that time through Fiscal Year 2013 Interior provided $257 billion to Federal, State and American Indian recipients. Out of the $257 billion collected since 1982 approximately $157 billion has gone to the general fund of the U.S. Treasury, $35 billion to the States and over $9 billion to American Indian communities.

Special purposes funds, like the Land and Water Conservation Fund, the National Historic Preservation Fund and the Reclamation Fund, have received over $56 billion.

I'd like to take a moment to mention how States and local governments have used their $35 billion which is truly significant.

Many States have developed formulas to return moneys to individual counties that may have been impacted by energy development. For instance, the State of Louisiana distributes the Federal funds between individual parishes for schools, local projects and the local governing authority for each parish.

In the Western part of the country, States use disbursements to fund their educational systems, infrastructure, correctional systems, water conservation and public safety.

At Interior we are always looking for ways to improve our collection and disbursement activities to benefit all American taxpayers, States and Indian communities. An example of our recent work includes regulatory changes for the Gulf of Mexico.

Back in 2006 the Gulf of Mexico Energy Security Act opened additional areas in the Gulf of Mexico for offshore oil and gas leasing. The act provides that 37.5 percent of the revenues for these new areas are distributed to the four Gulf of Mexico oil and gas producing States of Alabama, Louisiana, Mississippi and Texas and their coastal, political subdivisions and 12.5 percent to the Land and Water Conservation Fund.

Through proposed regulations that we published earlier this year, beginning in 2017 the act will share additional revenue from any new lease issued after December 20, 2006. The revenue would be shared in the same percentages as for the newly opened areas, 37.5 percent to the Gulf States and their coastal, political, subdivisions and 12.5 percent to the Land and Water Conservation Fund. However, this additional revenue sharing is subject to a cap of $500 million per year through 2055.

Any revenues in excess of this cap will go into the U.S. Treasury.

Madame Chair, all of us at the Department of Interior are committed to effectively managing these resources for the good of the American people and our Indian communities, who all share in their ownership. As we continue to move forward with executing our mission, we are committed to enhancing our royalty management program to ensure that the American public receives every dollar due.

Thank you for the opportunity to testify. I'd be happy to answer any questions that the committee may have.

[The prepared statement of Mr. Gould follows:]

PREPARED STATEMENT OF GREG GOULD, DIRECTOR, OFFICE OF NATURAL RESOURCES REVENUE, DEPARTMENT OF THE INTERIOR

*Introduction*

Madame Chairman Landrieu, Ranking Member Murkowski, and members of the Committee, I am pleased to appear before you today to discuss the impact of leveraging natural resource production as a revenue-generator and job-creator for States and local governments.

*Economic Impacts and Importance to State and Local Governments*

The Department of the Interior manages the public lands and Federal waters that provide resources critical to the Nation's energy security; is responsible for collecting and distributing revenue from energy development; and ensures that the American taxpayer receives a fair return for development of those Federal resources. The lands and resources managed by the Department are vast. Onshore, in the 33 states where there are Federal leases, over 36 million acres are under lease. Offshore, the Department has made 60 million acres available for development in the past three offshore lease sales alone. In just the Gulf of Mexico, there are over 32 million acres under active lease.

These onshore and offshore lands contribute to our nation's economy in large and small ways. According to the Department's 2013 Economic Contributions Report, a project that the Office of Policy Analysis led, the activities of the Department of the Interior contributed $360 billion to the U.S. economy in 2013, supporting 2 million jobs in activities including outdoor recreation and tourism, energy development, grazing, and timber harvest.

*The Leasing Process*

When individuals or companies lease Federal lands, they competitively bid and pay an initial bonus and annual rent for the right to explore and develop energy and mineral resources on the leased lands. If they find, extract, and sell minerals, the Federal Government is entitled to a certain percentage of-or royalty on-the production. In many cases, States and, sometimes, local governments receive a direct share of these revenues.

*Disbursements*

The Federal Government has been collecting leasing revenues from energy mineral production on Federal onshore lands since 1920; on American Indian lands since 1925; and on Federal offshore lands since 1953. In 1982, the Federal Oil and Gas Royalty Management Act (FOGRMA) created a comprehensive, consolidated system for the collection, accounting, and disbursement of these revenues. From 1982 through fiscal year 2013, Interior has provided $257.0 billion to Federal, State, and American Indian recipients through this program. Approximately 61 percent of all annual collections have gone to the General Fund of the U.S. Treasury, 22 percent to special purpose funds, 14 percent to States, and 3 percent to the American Indian community.

In fiscal year 2013, the Office of Natural Resources Revenue (ONRR) disbursed over $14.0 billion to the U.S. Treasury, various State and American Indian accounts, and special use accounts, such as the Land and Water Conservation Fund.

Special purpose funds, including the Land and Water Conservation Fund (LWCF), the National Historic Preservation Fund, and the Reclamation Fund, have received $56.5 billion in ONRR collected mineral revenues since 1982.

*Disbursements to States*

Revenues disbursed to States and local governments from energy and mineral development occurring on Federal lands within their borders are particularly important to many States today. They apply these revenues to a variety of local needs ranging from school funding to infrastructure improvements and water conservation projects. States have used Federal mineral revenues to build new schools, senior citizen facilities, and hospitals. In some cases, this money pays salaries for teachers, funds local road improvements, and provides grants for important local projects.

In Wyoming, for example, revenues that the State receives from energy production on Federal lands are generally distributed on a percentage basis. A portion of the money goes to the State general fund, the University Fund, the School Foundation (K-12,), the Highway Fund and county roads, cities, and towns based on population, School Capital Construction (K-12) and to the Budget Reserve.

The State of Louisiana distributes the Federal funds to individual Parishes for schools and other local projects: it distributes 50 percent to Parishes for schools, and 50 percent to the "Police Jury" (the local governing authority for each Parish), based on production that occurs in the local parishes.

In New Mexico, the State Land Office collects Federal royalties and, primarily, their distributions support education. Approximately 83 percent goes to public schools (K–12), which pays teacher salaries and provides overall operating funds. In addition to public schools, a portion of the money goes to Higher Education. A small percentage also goes to the correctional system.

Federal mineral lease revenues to the State of Colorado are distributed in a formula set in state statute. The State distributes Federal mineral lease revenues to education (K –12), local governments for operating and capital expenses, water conservation, and for higher education capital projects.

In Utah, a portion of the Federal disbursements goes to the Community Impact Board, which makes awards to local governments (in the form of grants or loans) for various projects, including infrastructure, water and sewer, and public safety. A portion of the funds are returned to the county of origin.

Many other States benefit in a similar manner from the revenue that the Department of theInterior collects and disburses.

*Revenue Distribution*

The distribution of revenue is governed by statute and varies by land type, as follows:

- Onshore mineral leasing receipts from public domain lands leased under Mineral Leasing Act (MLA)[1] authority disburse at a rate of 49 percent to the States, 40 percent to the Reclamation Fund for western water projects, and 11 percent to the General Fund of theU.S. Treasury. Alaska receives 88.2 percent of mineral leasing receipts for Mineral Leasing Act lands.
- The collections from State Select Lands disburse at a rate of 90 percent to the States and 10 percent to the General Fund of the U.S. Treasury. Alaska receives 100 percent of mineral leasing receipts from State Select Lands.
- The collections from geothermal production disburse at a rate of 50 percent to the States, 25 percent to the county, and 25 percent to the General Fund of the U.S. Treasury.
- Collections from the National Petroleum Reserve in Alaska disburse at a rate of 50 percent to Alaska and 50 percent to the General Fund of the U.S. Treasury.

  —The Energy Policy Act of 1992, P.L. 102–486, requires the Secretary of the Interior to disburse monthly to States all mineral leasing payments authorized by Section 6 of the Mineral Leasing Act for Acquired Lands. Therefore, the Department distributes:

  —Collections from lands acquired for flood control, navigation, and allied purposes, transferring 25 percent of the total to the General Fund of the U.S. Treasury and 75 percent to the States.

  —Collections from National Forest Lands, transferring 75 percent to the Forest Service and 25 percent to the States.

- Outer Continental Shelf (OCS) receipts, including rents, bonuses, and royalties, are the main funding source for the mandated $900 million required to be deposited annually in the Land and Water Conservation Fund (LWCF). OCS receipts also provide $150 million in funding for the Historic Preservation Fund. Of the remaining OCS receipts, the majority are deposited into the general fund of the U.S. Treasury.
- The Gulf of Mexico Energy Security Act of 2006 (GOMESA, P.L. 109–432) opened additional areas in the Gulf of Mexico for offshore oil and gas leasing. The Act provided that 50 percent of revenues from these open areas (termed "qualified OCS revenues") disburse to four Gulf of Mexico oil and gas producing States (Alabama, Louisiana, Mississippi, and Texas) and their Coastal Political Subdivisions (CPSs) and to the Land and Water Conservation Fund, with specific provisions for allocation during fiscal years 2007–2016. Beginning in 2017, the Act would allocate additional revenue to these States, their CSPs, and the LWCF from any new leases signed after enactment in the current program areas of the Gulf. The revenue would be shared in the same percentages (37.5 percent to Gulf States and their CPSs and 12.5 percent to LWCF) in the newly opened areas, and payments are similarly made in the year following the revenue collection. However, this additional revenue sharing is subject to a cap of $500 million per year (through 2055); revenues in excess of this cap would continue to go to the U.S. Treasury. The National Park Service (NPS) currently administers GOMESA funds allocated to LWCF State grants.
- Under Section 8(g) of the OCS Lands Act, payments are also made to coastal States for an area known as the 8(g) zone, which is the area approximately three miles seaward from the State/Federal boundary. States receive 27 percent of OCS collections within the 8(g) zone.

---

[1] Section 302 of the Bipartisan Budget Act of 2013 directs the Department to deduct 2 percent from the amount payable to each State in fiscal year 2014 and each year thereafter. Percentages shown in the text have been adjusted to reflect this deduction.

*ONRR Background*

Within the Department of the Interior, ONRR is responsible for collecting, disbursing, and verifying Federal and Indian energy and other natural resource revenues on behalf of all Americans.

ONRR's 2010 reorganization into the Office of the Secretary provided an opportunity for a strategic review to improve the management and oversight of revenue collection and disbursement activities for the Department. We institutionalized our employee-driven continuous improvement process by implementing semiannual prioritization discussions, requesting regular employee input, and integrating recommendations into day-to-day mission work.

ONRR's goal is to be a world-class natural resources revenue management program, setting the standard for accountability and transparency. We are focused on implementing priority initiatives aligned with our strategic goals to achieve:

- Timely and accurate revenues and data distributed to recipients.
- Timely compliance from companies and payment of every dollar due.
- Trust in ONRR's professionalism, integrity, efficiency, and quality.

*Conclusion*

Madame Chairman, the Department of the Interior manages these Federal resources for the good of the American people, who all share in their ownership. As we continue to move forward with executing our mission, we are committed to enhancing our royalty management program to ensure that the American public receives every dollar due. Thank you for the opportunity to testify. I am happy to answer any questions that the Committee may have.

The CHAIR. Alright.

We're going to each ask one question and then take a break and come back to finish our questioning, if you don't mind, Director. Then take our second panel.

I'd like to put up on the easel though, a couple of charts that I brought as well. Please put these up, the charts, please.

This is the Federal land receipts by source since 1985. The reason I'm pointing this out is because while the numbers are impressive from one perspective when you talk about the total amounts of money reinvested. My calculation is that all of the revenues collected from 1985 and we're using the 1985 start date just for the purposes of this hearing, comparing apples to apples. From 1985 to the present time the total revenues from all sources is about two hundred and $48 billion.

Is that your record?

Mr. GOULD. That's correct. Yes.

The CHAIR. Approximately? OK.

Mr. GOULD. That's close.

The CHAIR. Interestingly, that is how much the Federal Government collects in 1 year from corporate income tax. So in some ways it sounds like a really big number, but in some ways it's a really small revenue stream for the Federal Government. It's a huge revenue stream or lack of revenue stream for local communities in Alaska, Louisiana, Gulf Coast States, but it's relatively a small stream of revenue.

So one could ask, since it's just a small, you know, over from 1985, the whole amount, equals 1 year of corporate revenue. Why couldn't we share more of it with the local communities? It's a very interesting question.

For instance, in Louisiana last year offshore, just Louisiana, there are four producing States in the Gulf, but Louisiana share territory is the largest and the most productive. It's actually responsible for 80 percent of the offshore production. Last year your office, ONRR, collected $9 billion. Eighty percent of that came from offshore Louisiana, roughly. Yet the State received only $297 thousand.

Do you think that's in line with any revenue sharing bill that this country has ever put forward whether it was—any, any comparable to that considering the Western States keep about 50 percent of their funding?

Mr. GOULD. So as the Director of the Office of Natural Resource Revenue, my job is to make sure that we collect, verify and then disburse the appropriate revenues as dictated by both the statute and regulation.

The CHAIR. But let me ask you this. Is there any State that receives less revenue relative to what they produce than Louisiana? Do you know?

Mr. GOULD. Relative to production? I don't know that exact number, but I can definitely look that up for you.

The CHAIR. OK. I think you'd be hard pressed to find another State that produces more and receives less even though we've made progress with GOMESA and passed it. But we have this arbitrary cap. We had to press the funding back for budget issues.

But you wonder what budget issues could really be that significant given that 1 year of corporate income tax equals the total amount of revenues collected in all streams since 1985. What could possibly be pressing the budget that much that would short change these production States in such a dramatic way?

Senator Murkowski.

Senator MURKOWSKI. Just very quickly, Madame Chair, because I know we've—we're running on the tail end of the votes.

I just want to make sure that my facts are accurate when we go back to, kind of, the history of where we got here with revenue sharing.

In your written testimony you State that between 1982 through FY2013 Interior has provided $257 billion to Federal, State and American Indian recipients through the program. So is it correct to assume that that was when this whole, the concept, of revenue sharing to the States began, was 1982 or was it prior to then?

Some have suggested that what Senator Landrieu and I are proposing with additional revenue sharing to the States, particularly offshore, is that this is a brand new concept. Can you give me a little bit of the background here? Are my dates right?

Mr. GOULD. Your dates are right in terms of the—my testimony and the period for that amount of money.

In terms of revenue sharing it dates back to the Mineral Leasing Act in 1820, I believe was when that was passed. So revenue sharing has been a concept that's been part of our regulations and part of our statutes for almost a century.

Senator MURKOWSKI. That's onshore. Offshore the history would begin when?

Mr. GOULD. With the OCS Lands Act in 1976, I believe.

Senator MURKOWSKI. So more of a quarter of a century for offshore and century plus for onshore, this concept of revenue sharing to the States and to our tribes.

Mr. GOULD. Correct.

Senator MURKOWSKI. Has been something that we have done historically.

Madame Chairman, I'll have one more quick question for the Director when we come back.

Mr. GOULD. Actually a point of clarification.

I think it was in 1986 when you were sharing the AG portion of the OCS Lands Act, revenues with the States.

Senator MURKOWSKI. The HE, yes.

Mr. GOULD. The AG. It's that 3 mile area.

The CHAIR. The AG is the line between 3 and 6 miles that we, sort of, cleaned up the boundary.

Senator MURKOWSKI. Right.

The CHAIR. I'll talk about that when I get back in a minute.

We're going to go vote.

But please be prepared to break down that $247 billion into timber, minerals, oil, gas, coal, grazing, etcetera because we want to get those numbers on the record.

Thank you.

We'll take a break for 30 minutes. Recess.

Mr. GOULD. Thank you.

The CHAIR. The committee will stand in recess.

[RECESS]

The CHAIR. The Energy and Natural Resources Committee will come out of recess and continue our hearing on Leveraging America's Resources as Revenue Generators and Job Creators.

We had an opening statement from both myself and Senator Murkowski, then opening statement from Director Gould. We're now into the period of questioning.

But before I do I wanted to go to a few graphs up here where we left off.

From 1985 for the purposes of this hearing to get apples to apples and oranges to oranges, we're starting with the 1985 date.

You testified, Director, that we had raised how much money overall? Two hundred and?

Mr. GOULD. Two Hundred and Fifty-two billion.

The CHAIR. Fifty-two billion. Could you break those down into the main categories, please?

Mr. GOULD. So, and my numbers again are back to 1982. I'm sorry to say we are going to have our staff try and get the numbers to match your 1985 numbers.

Mr. GOULD. Also the Office of Natural Resource Revenue, we don't collect the grazing fees, the boat rentals and all, BLM and Park Service and other offices. I've got contacts back to them to start looking up that data for you.

Mr. GOULD. I can give you the numbers for royalties associated with coal, $13.4 billion since 1982.

Royalties associated with natural gas, $87.7 billion.

The CHAIR. Is that onshore or off or both?

Mr. GOULD. That's total.

The CHAIR. Could you break it down onshore and off, please?

Mr. GOULD. OK, so for coal it's obviously onshore and the coal is $697.4 million.

The CHAIR. Wait, I'm sorry, you had 13.4 for coal.

Mr. GOULD. That's—and then American Indian land makes up the balance of 78.2.

I'm sorry, I only have those breakouts by Fiscal Year 2013.

The CHAIR. OK.

Mr. GOULD. I don't have the totals by—is that correct?

So I can't break off onshore and offshore with me right now by that total accumulative, I don't think.

The CHAIR. OK. For the record it's really important for us to break down these revenues.

Mr. GOULD. Yes.

The CHAIR. Because that's what this committee is very interested in is not only how much is generated but in what way and where are they generated.

Mr. GOULD. Yes.

The CHAIR. Then we're going to get to how they're distributed and how they're used which is the undergirding information for this important hearing.

Mr. GOULD. Correct.

The CHAIR. So your office, since it was created, is focused on collecting these revenues, keeping a record of these revenues and you have partners in the Federal Government where you can get additional information.

Mr. GOULD. That's correct.

The CHAIR. OK, if you would submit all of that information before the last—the next 2 weeks that would be helpful.

Now, are you responsible for timber harvest on BLM lands?

Mr. GOULD. No, ma'am.

The CHAIR. Alright. Who is responsible for timber harvest on BLM land?

Mr. GOULD. BLM is.

The CHAIR. OK. Alrighty.

I think that my questions for you are done. Thank you, Mr. Gould. We'll introduce the next panel.

Mr. GOULD. Thank you, Madame Chair.

The CHAIR. Thank you very much.

As the next panel comes forward and we're going to try to wrap up our hearing about 12:30 or quarter to one. So we want to ask everyone to be as succinct as possible. I'll introduce them as they're going to speak.

First, the Honorable Charlotte Randolph, President of Lafourche Parish served for over 6 years as a citizen activist before being elected Parish President. She's the first female president in Lafourche Parish history. Has been one of the leaders against Parishes Against Coastal Erosion, the PACE organization.

This organization represents over 2 million people in Southern Louisiana fighting for significantly higher share of royalty money from oil and gas revenues to protect and sustain our coast.

Next we'll have Paul Pearce, President of the National Forestry Council and School Coalition. Mr. Pearce, it was good to see you, I think, recently. You are responsible for advocating for Federal funding for Secure Rural Schools, County Payments and advocating for the Federal forest management, prior to that you were a county commissioner in the State of Washington.

Joel Webster, Director, Center for Western Lands, the Theodore Roosevelt Conservation Partnership. Joel is the Director of that organization. He joined in 2007, has spent the past decade working along hunting and fishing groups, wildlife managers, decisionmakers and agency leaders to shape Federal, public lands policy. Welcome, Mr. Webster.

Sean Shafer, Consulting Manager of Quest Offshore Resources. Sean manages as a full service marketing research and consulting firm focused on offshore oil and gas, for the offshore oil and gas industry. In this position he leads the production of specialized market reports to these operators and is in a good position to give us some insight into what the future may hold in that area offshore.

Dr. Laura Nelson, Office of Energy Development, has significant experience in government relations, permitting, power planning. She was Vice President of Energy and Environmental at Red Leaf Resources from 2007 to 2012. She was—served as Energy Advisor to the Utah Governor, John Huntsman.

Then finally, we have Duane Taylor, Director of Federal Affairs, Motorcycle Industry Council and I'll put some additional remarks for you, Mr. Taylor in the record.

The CHAIR. Thank you all for being here.

Ms. Randolph, we'll start with you, please. If we can limit this to 5 minutes each and then we'll have a round of questions.

Thank you so much.

## STATEMENT OF CHARLOTTE A. RANDOLPH, PRESIDENT, LAFOURCHE PARISH, THIBODAUX, LO

Ms. RANDOLPH. Thank you, Chair Landrieu, Ranking Member Murkowski and members of the committee for the opportunity to testify before you today on how parishes and counties are leveraging America's resources as a revenue generator and job creator.

My name is Charlotte Randolph. I'm the President of Lafourche Parish, in the State of Louisiana. Our population is about 98,000 people.

I'm also proud to represent the National Association of Counties. NACo is the only national organization that represents county governments in the United States including Alaska's boroughs and Louisiana's parishes. Founded in 1935, NACo assists America's 3,069 counties in pursuing excellence in public service to produce healthy, vibrant, safe and resilient counties.

I'm here today to discuss how revenues generated from our Nation's natural resources should be shared with parishes and counties. Revenue sharing whether from oil and gas production, timber, renewable energy or other types of natural resources can be a central component of a county's revenue stream. How counties can use natural resource revenues can vary widely.

Some States the counties must use those revenues for construction and maintenance of county roads. Other States dictate that local governments must use natural resource revenues for public schools, transportation and retirement funds are our county's general fund.

My testimony will discuss these points. In particular, energy production significantly impacts communities and local governments. Natural resource production is critical to Lafourche Parish. Lafourche Parish is critical to natural resource production.

Domestic energy production is a major component of our economy. It directly and indirectly generates tens of thousands of jobs which in turn generate millions of dollars to our local community and State.

In 2013 approximately $2.8 billion came from the sale of new oil and gas leases in the Federal waters off Louisiana's coast in the Gulf of Mexico. These areas remain the Nation's primary offshore source of oil and gas, generating about 97 percent of all Outer Continental Shelf production. In fact, this makes Louisiana the second largest producer of crude oil and the second largest producer of natural gas in these United States.

Port Fourchon, our Lafourche Parish port services 90 percent of the deep water drilling structures located in the Gulf region. In fact the port is now in the final phase of an expansion project which will more than double its size and accommodate the growing needs of the oil and gas industry. Further, the Louisiana Offshore Oil Port, LOOP, located 14 miles off our coast provides tanker offloading for some of the largest tankers in the world. They handle about 13 percent of the foreign oil and connects the Nation's only deep water port to more than 50 percent of the Nation's refining capacity.

Blessed with abundant resources Lafourche Parish plays a pivotal role in our national energy policy. But people require services that the parishes provide including law enforcement and courts, emergency management, infrastructure maintenance and development and environmental protection to name just a few. While to some degree or other most counties provide these basic services. There are additional services we provide that directly relate to our natural resource industries.

Infrastructure is a prime example. Counties own about 45 percent of public roads. Natural resources counties, we build and maintain the roads, bridges and ports that enable people to access the natural resources. Revenue sharing enables counties to keep these facilities in good repair and the economy moving.

LA Highway 1 in Lafourche Parish is a 50 year old road to LOOP and to Fourchon. It's been designated a high priority corridor on the National Highway system because of its role as critical energy infrastructure. The road needs to be maintained and expanded. We borrowed $175 million in addition to some State and Federal funding to complete a portion of this road, but we need $315 million more to complete the highway.

These local challenges can have national impacts. A recent economic study found that if Highway 1 were to be washed out due to a natural disaster, rebuilding the unimproved portion could take 90 days. That would result in $7.8 billion loss in the Gross Domestic Product.

The same study also revealed that a week disruption to Louisiana's pipeline system would raise gasoline prices by almost 22 cents a gallon. Over a week period this translates into a $1.7 billion cost to consumers. That's at $60 a barrel. Oil is now at $100 a barrel.

In conclusion, madame chair, I commend you and the committee for holding this hearing and examining the impact of how we can leverage our natural resources to generate revenue and create jobs.

Thank you.

[The prepared statement of Ms. Randolph follows:]

PREPARED STATEMENT OF CHARLOTTE A. RANDOLPH, PRESIDENT, LAFOURCHE
PARISH, THIBODAUX, LO

Thank you Chair Landrieu, Ranking Member Murkowski and Members of the Committee for the opportunity to testify before you today on how parishes and counties are leveraging America's resources as a revenue generator and job creator.

My name is Charlotte Randolph, and I am the President, or elected Chief Executive Officer, of Lafourche Parish in the state of Louisiana. Lafourche Parish serves a population of 97,029, is comprised of 1,472 square miles and is situated in south eastern Louisiana on the coast of the Gulf of Mexico.

I am also proud to represent the National Association of Counties (NACo). NACo is the only national organization that represents county governments in the United States, including Alaska's boroughs and Louisiana's parishes. Founded in 1935, NACo assists America's 3,069 counties in pursuing excellence in public service to produce healthy, vibrant, safe and resilient counties. NACo promotes sound public policies, fosters county solutions and innovation, promotes intergovernmental and public-private collaboration and provides value-added services to save counties and taxpayers money.

I am here today to discuss how revenues generated from our nation's natural resources should be shared with parishes and counties. Revenue sharing-whether for oil and gas production, timber, renewable energy, or other types of natural resources- can be an essential component of a county's revenue stream. Whether counties are allotted revenue from natural resources may depend on state laws. Additionally, how counties can use natural resource(s) revenues can vary widely. For example, in some states, the counties must use revenues for construction and maintenance of county roads. Other states dictate that local governments must use natural resource revenues for public schools, transportation, retirement funds and/or a county's general fund.

My testimony will discuss three key points;

1. The importance of natural resource production to Lafourche Parish, Louisiana

2. Energy production significantly impacts communities and local governments

3. The Federal government should proportionally share revenue generated by energy development to support of local infrastructure

1. Natural resource production is critical to Lafourche Parish and Lafourche Parish is crittee to natural resource production! Domestic energy production is a major component of the economy in Lafourche Parish. It directly, and indirectly, generates tens of thousands of jobs which in turn generate millions of dollars to our local community and state. In 2013, approximately $2.8 billion dollars alone came from the sale of new oil and gas leases in the federal waters off Louisiana's coast in the Gulf of Mexico. These areas remain the nation's primary offshore source of oil and gas, generating about 97 percent of all Outer Continental Shelf production. In fact, this makes Louisiana the second largest producer of crude oil and the second largest producer of natural gas among the 50 states.

Port Fourchon, our Lafourche Parish's port, services 90 percent of the deep water drilling structures located in the Gulf region. In fact, the port is now in the final phase of an expansion project which will more than double its size and accommodate the growing needs of the oil and gas industry.

Further, the Louisiana Offshore Oil Port (LOOP), located 14 miles off the coast near Port Fourchon, provides tanker offloading for some of the largest tankers in the world. LOOP handles 13 percent of the foreign oil and connects the nation's only deep water port to more than 50 percent of the nation's refining capacity.

Blessed with abundant natural resources, Lafourche Parish plays a pivotal role in our national energy policy.

2. Energy production significantly impacts communities and local governments.—
In Lafourche Parish, we have benefited significantly from having so many jobs directly related to the production of oil and gas. For example, median household income in our parish (between 2008 and 2012) was 13 percent higher than the state average ($50,573 vs $44,673).

This is clearly a net positive for our community, but you must remember that people require services that the parish provide-including law enforcement and courts, emergency management, infrastructure maintenance and development, and environmental protection, to name just a few. While to some degree or another most counties provide these basic services, there are additional services we provide that directly relate to our natural resource industries.

Infrastructure is the prime example-counties own 45 percent of the public roads in 43 states. And in natural resources counties, we build and maintain the roads, bridges and ports that enable people to access the natural resources and get them to market-helping to ensure that our nation is globally competitive. Revenue sharing enables counties to keep these facilities in good repair and the economy moving. This is especially important for counties in rural areas. You should remember that of the nation's 3,069 counties, 50 percent (1,542) serve counties with populations below 25,000 residents.

Louisiana Highway 1 in Lafourche Parish is a 50-year old road to LOOP, has been designated a High Priority Corridor on the National Highway System, because of its role as a "critical energy infrastructure." It is imperative that we maintain and expand Highway 1. While we have been able to secure some state and federal funding to build a portion, we have borrowed $175 million to complete this section. We need another $315 million to complete the highway to this nationally significant port.

These local challenges can have national impacts. A recent economic study found that if Highway 1 were to be washed out due to a natural disaster, rebuilding the unimproved portion of the highway could take up to ninety days. This could result in a $7.8 billion loss in the Gross Domestic Product. The same study also revealed that "a three-week disruption to Louisiana's pipeline system would raise gasoline prices by 21.6 cents per gallon nationwide. Over a three-week period, this translates into a $1.74 billion cost to consumers." That is with oil at $66 a barrel. Today's oil price is well over $100.

Additionally, it must be said that oil and gas activities have taken a toll on barrier islands and coastal zones, lowering coastal communities' protection from storms, as evidenced by Hurricanes Katrina, Gustav and Ike. Coastal parishes and counties want to take action to protect and restore valuable coastal wetlands and affected areas but simply are not able to generate sufficient resources to do so on their own.

3. The Federal Government should proportionally share natural resources revenue with affected parishes and counties.—Lafourche Parish and NACo strongly support responsible development of our nation's natural resources. Such development can, and does, build strong local economies while generating enormous revenues for the federal treasury. However, any economic activity requires local infrastructure which is built and maintained at the local level.

Specifically, NACo supports amending the Federal Mineral Leasing Act so that an additional five percent from the federal portion of mineral lease revenue would be returned to the county from which the mineral was extracted. NACo also supports sharing federal leasing and rights-of-way revenues from renewable energy development (wind, solar, and geothermal) and federal Stewardship Contracts on federal lands with county governments where that development and contracts occurs. In addition, NACo supports the historic 25 percent national forest revenue sharing and we encourage you to extend the Secure Rural Schools Program as a bridge to more sustainable landscape scale forest management.

In conclusion, it is critical that the federal government share natural resource development revenues proportionally with the counties that support and are affected by that development-as they are responsible for the needs of the citizens they serve.

Madam Chair, I commend you and the Committee for holding this hearing and examining the impact of how we can leverage our natural resources to generate revenue and create jobs. Counties, parishes and boroughs across the country play a key role in natural resource stewardship and development and look for your continued leadership to ensure that we have a strong federal-state-local partnership. Local communities depend on robust federal revenue sharing to help their citizens and ensure the economic viability of our nation.

As you take steps to examine existing revenue sharing programs, we look forward to working with you in the future.

The CHAIR. Thank you very much.

Mr. Pearce.

## STATEMENT OF PAUL PEARCE, PRESIDENT, NATIONAL FOREST COUNTIES AND SCHOOLS COALITION, STEVENSON, WA

Mr. PEARCE. Thank you.

Madame Chair Landrieu, Ranking Member Murkowski and Senators on behalf of counties, parishes, boroughs and schools impacted by national forests, we thank you for this opportunity to testify on the success of SRS and on production within the forests.

We wish to thank Chair Landrieu for your comment at the National Association of County meetings 2 weeks ago on SRS and PILT where you expressed support for continued funding of both payments. Thank you very much.

We thank Ranking Member Murkowski for her hard work over the many years on forest health issues and SRS bridge funding.

The revenue sharing contract between the U.S. Government and counties worked well into the early 1990s when court decisions and endangered species listings, agency priorities, dramatically reduced extraction activities on public lands including timber. In 1992 Congress created OWL Guarantee moneys for the 51 counties impacted by the Northern Spotted Owl. The listing and critical habitat designation has accounted for the loss of 30 thousand jobs between 1992 and 2012.

In 2000 Congress passed the Secure Rural Schools Act which was reauthorized through Fiscal Year 2013. SRS must be reauthorized this Fiscal Year or we face a devastating loss of over $240 million in revenue to these rural counties and schools. We do respectfully request that any SRS reauthorization contain new language which replaces the current cumbersome formula with a statement, "All counties opting to receive a portion of the State payment will receive an amount equal to their Fiscal Year 2010 payment." Fairness for all.

There are many who believe that SRS payments have decoupled sustainable timber harvest and revenue sharing programs to counties and schools. We disagree. As actual shared receipts are the first dollars you use to pay SRS each year, these receipts accounted for $58 million in Fiscal Year 2013.

SRS contains 3 titles. All of which have been successful for counties and schools.

Title I is direct payments to county roads and schools.

In a handful of counties these funds are available to support public health, law enforcement and other services. In many counties these are the majority of their road funds. The fact is counties are responsible for 45 percent of the roads and 39 percent of the bridges in the United States.

The impact of these moneys on many rural schools is the district remaining open or closing their doors.

Dr. Eyler, an economist, reports the result of losing SRS is $1.3 billion in sales, $187 or $178 million in taxes, over 10,000 additional jobs including more than 3,000 in education and 1,400 in counties.

Title II our money is used for forest projects utilizing Resource Advisory Committees or RACs which have consistently proven to be the most successful collaborative entities nationally for over a decade, other than the Clearwater in Idaho which has been a national icon.

A few examples include Louisiana on the Kisatchie National Forest. RAC moneys leveraged local funds and secured completion of road repair, protecting endangered species, water quality and safe access to public recreation.

Sitka, Alaska. RAC funds a science mentor program partnering high school students with Forest Service, Fish and Game and University of Alaska to collect and analyze data on the Tongass National Forest.

Washington on the Gifford Pinchot Forest, Forest Youth Success employs 40 kids and crew leaders to work doing a multitude of projects throughout the forest. It's a partnership between schools, WSU extension, counties and the Forest Service.

Title III funds are a reimbursement for emergency services like search and rescue, community wildfire planning and fire wise implementation.

Examples of just two searches in 2012 in my home county include a hiker who fell into Mount St. Helens' crater eventually costing local, State and Federal agencies over $150,000 .

The second involved a 2-week search for a young woman lost in the Columbia River gorge costing local, State and Federal agencies $550 thousand.

Without Title III the counties could not absorb these costs.

We pledge to work to assist in enactment of legislation that provides continued bridge funding to forestry counties and schools but believe that long term, economic vitality must include active, sustainable forest management including sustainable timber harvests to achieve resilient forests, lands, jobs and economic vitality.

We have been working with the LWCF coalition, NACo and a number of other partners on trying to find agreement where SRS, PILT, LWCF might be fully funded, long term.

Thank you very much for this opportunity to appear before you and comment on the future and current success of SRS, a program that we must reauthorize.

Thank you.

The CHAIR. Thank you, Mr. Pearce.

Mr. Webster.Joel Webster, Director, Center for Western Lands, Theodore Roosevelt Conservation Partnership, Missoula, MT

## STATEMENT OF JOEL WEBSTER, DIRECTOR, CENTER FOR WESTERN LANDS, THEODORE ROOSEVELT CONSERVATION PARTNERSHIP, MISSOULA, MT

Mr. WEBSTER. Madame Chairwoman Landrieu, Ranking Member Murkowski and members of the committee, thank you very much for the opportunity to testify.

My name is Joel Webster. I am the Director of the Center for Western Lands at the Theodore Roosevelt Conservation Partnership, a national conservation organization that is working to guarantee every American quality places to hunt and fish. We work with 36 partner organizations that represent the wide spectrum of the hunting and fishing community.

America's natural resources are the infrastructure of a robust, outdoor recreation economy.

One, that according to a 2012 Outdoor Industry Association report, accounts for $646 billion in direct consumer spending and more than 6 million jobs. Never has the phrase, Made in the USA, been so accurate. American jobs in industries rely on America's natural resources. They cannot be exported but they do run the risk of being downsized if investments in the conservation and access are not prioritized.

Hunting and fishing activities are not only a valued part of America's heritage, but a significant contributor to the outdoor economy. Thirty-seven million Americans hunt and fish and spend $58 billion annually.

While recreational activities like hunting and fishing might appear to be expendable or mere pastimes, they're vital everyday activities to those communities that rely on that business.

To the tackle shop owner in Cocodrie, Louisiana, who sells bait, ice and fuel, fishing is not a pastime. It will send a kid to college.

For the outfitter based in Fairbanks, Alaska, who relies on booking trips for caribou hunts, hunting is not expendable, it pays the mortgage.

I'd like to share a quick personal study—story. In 1961 my grandfather and a friend hired public lands outfitters, who took them on a hunting trip of their lives. On this trip my grandfather traveled into the Bridger-Teton National Forest in Wyoming where he harvested a bull elk, a buck mule deer and a bear.

He wasn't a rich man, but between all the goods and services his trip required he spent a significant amount of his hard earned money. Years later my father would allocate his discretionary income to fund his own public lands hunting, fishing adventures. Fortunately I became the lucky recipient of a long standing and sustainable hunting and fishing tradition.

I've been able to spend the past 30 years of my life hunting with my father, friends and colleagues. Last year for a 2-month hunting season, I spent about $3,500 bucks on fuel, licenses, food and hunting gear. When you look at the big picture the recreational activity of 37 million individual hunters and anglers adds up.

These benefits do not stop with direct consumer spending and jobs. These activities generate $39.9 billion in Federal tax revenue and $39.7 billion in State and local taxes. In fact, sportsmen have long understood the intersection between conservation and hunting and fishing.

Through the Pittman-Robertson and Dingell-Johnson Federal excise taxes on guns, ammunition, fishing tackle, boats and fuel which are invested back into our natural resources, sportsman have been paying their own way for the better part of a century which leads me to a bigger point. Conservation of our natural resources is the critical first step in maintaining the vitality of the hunting and fishing economy.

Our natural resources take many forms. But a tangible example for me, as a Westerner, is the value of our Federal/public lands. These lands help drive the economic engines of rural communities and are where the large majority of western sportsmen hunt.

According to the U.S. Fish and Wildlife Service, 72 percent of all hunters from the Pacific and Mountain West hunt on public lands. Each summer and fall sportsmen crowd towns like Meeker, Colorado, Elko, Nevada, Salmon, Idaho, Cody, Wyoming and La Grande, Oregon to hunt and fish. They happily spend their hard earned money on vehicles, sporting goods, food, fuel, lodging, outfitters and guides. These sportsmen and the local economies depend on public lands for hunting and fishing.

Just as conservation of our resources is paramount, ensuring access to these places is also a necessity. There needs to be a commitment to providing public access to public lands. A 2000 report to the House Appropriations Committee concluded that more than 35 million acres of BLM and U.S. Forest Service land had inadequate access.

Proposed legislation such as making public lands public in the Hunt Act would dedicate 1.5 percent of the Land and Water Conservation Fund, an important program in itself, to provide public access to currently landlocked public lands.

In closing $646 billion in direct consumer spending and more than $6 million in American jobs rely on the conservation and responsible management of our natural resources. It is vital that decisionmakers commit themselves to reinvesting in public access and priority fish and wildlife habitat to support the sustainable outdoor recreation economy.

Thank you very much for the opportunity to testify. I look forward to working with you on these issues moving forward. I'd be happy to answer any questions.

[The prepared statement of Mr. Webster follows:]

PREPARED STATEMENT OF JOEL WEBSTER, DIRECTOR, CENTER FOR WESTERN LANDS, THEODORE ROOSEVELT CONSERVATION PARTNERSHIP, MISSOULA, MT

Chair Landrieu, Ranking Member Murkowski, and Members of the Committee, thank you very much for the opportunity to testify. My name is Joel Webster, and I am the Director of the Center for Western Lands at the Theodore Roosevelt Conservation Partnership, a national conservation organization that is dedicated to guaranteeing every American quality places to hunt and fish. We work with 36 partner organizations that represent the wide spectrum of hunting and fishing activities and conservation interests across the sporting community.

I have been asked to testify regarding the potential for America's natural resources to generate revenue and create jobs. Specifically, I am here to highlight the importance of Federal public lands in generating revenue and jobs through hunting and fishing related activities.

I'd like to start with a short story. In 1961, my grandfather and a friend hired a public lands outfitter who took them on the hunting trip of their lives. On this trip, my grandfather traveled into the Thoroughfare country of the Bridger-Teton National Forest in Wyoming where he harvested a bull elk, a buck mule deer and a bear. He wasn't a rich man, but between all the goods and services his trip required, he spent a significant amount on his hard-earned money. Years later, my father would allocate his discretionary income to fund his own public lands hunting and fishing adventures.

I grew up as a boy staring at the bear rug on my grandfather's wall, asking him about the trip and imagining what it must have been like to experience the land and wildlife up close. I was eager to set out on a similar adventure. Fortunately, I became the lucky recipient of a long-standing and sustainable hunting and fishing tradition. I've been able to spend the past thirty years of my life hunting with my father, friends and colleagues. All of us spend a large portion of our discretionary incomes on hunting and fishing gear, licenses and hunting trips. And we do so every year with enthusiasm for what we hope will be a life-long pursuit.

Thirty-seven million sportsmen enjoy the valued American tradition of hunting and fishing. And while these 37 million sportsmen derive personal benefits from a pastime they love, these sportsmen also provide a sustainable influx of money into the economy. According to a 2012 Outdoor Industry Association report, sportsmen pump $58 billion annually into the US economy. Hunting and fishing are a critical part of the American outdoor recreation economy, which generates $646 billion annually, supports 6.1 million jobs, and generates $39.9 billion in Federal tax revenue and $39.7 billion in state/local tax revenue.

Every summer and fall, sportsmen crowd towns like Meeker, Colorado; Elko, Nevada; Munising Michigan, Salmon, Idaho; Cody, Wyoming; and La Grande, Oregon to hunt and fish, and they happily spend their hard earned money on vehicles, sporting goods, food, fuel, lodging, and outfitters and guides. According to the US Fish and Wildlife Service, 72 percent of all hunters from the pacific and mountain west hunt on public lands. These sportsmen and the local economies depend on public lands for hunting and fishing.

Federal public lands help feed this economic engine. In order to sustain and continue building the outdoor economy and hunting and fishing opportunities, decisionmakers, non-government partners, and the public must make a long-term commitment: support the responsible management of Federal public lands and invest back into these lands.

First, there needs to be a commitment to providing public access to public lands. A 2004 report to the House Appropriations Committee concluded that more than 35 million acres of BLM and US Forest Service land have inadequate access. Proposed legislation such as Making Public Lands Public, would dedicate 1.5 percent of the Land and Water Conservation Fund-an important program in itself-to provide public access to currently landlocked public lands.

Second, in order to maintain the hunting and fishing participation that plays such a vital role in this economic engine, fish and wildlife habitat needs on public lands should be met through conservation policies that safeguard priority habitats, and through active management such as habitat restoration and enhancement.

Active habitat management is an industry in itself. A 2013 study conducted by Southwick Associates found that in 2012, $38.8 billion dollars was invested into Natural Resources Conservation (such as forest, fisheries and wildlife resources) by corporations, private donors, non-profits, and the government at the Federal, State, and local levels. That $38 billion dollars generated $12.9 billion in Federal and state tax revenues, fostered $93.2 billion in total economic activity and supported 660,000 jobs across the United States. These activities support fish and wildlife habitats and help to sustain the hunting and fishing economy in America.

In closing, if we want continued public hunting and fishing and a strong and sustainable outdoor recreation-based economy, we need to retain and responsibly manage Federal public lands and put forth a strong investment in public access and natural resource conservation. Thank you very much for the opportunity to testify. I look forward to working with you on these issues moving forward. I would be happy to answer any questions you might have.

The CHAIR. Thank you, Mr. Webster, for that personal and passionate testimony. Appreciate it.

Mr. Shafer.

## STATEMENT OF SEAN SHAFER, CONSULTING MANAGER, QUEST OFFSHORE RESOURCES, INC., SUGAR LAND, TX

Mr. SHAFER. Thank you, Chairman Landrieu, Ranking Member Murkowski, members of the committee. My name is Sean Shafer. I would like to thank you for the opportunity to testify before the committee.

Just to give you a brief overview I'm going to focus on the economic impact of the oil and gas industry in the U.S. and especially on the impact of opening up new areas of the OCS.

The Nation's oil and gas industry supports 9.8 million U.S. jobs and 8 percent of the U.S. economy. Approximately 2.6 million of the jobs are directly within the industry. Due to their on average, higher paying nature, many jobs within the industry tend to have larger effects on overall employment throughout the economy. Additionally the oil and natural gas industry has been at the forefront of the Nation's economic recovery, experiencing job growth at a significantly faster rate than the rest of the economy.

From 2007 to 2012 oil and gas employment grew 40 percent compared to overall employment's 1 percent growth, accounting to around 160,000 of the one million new jobs created. These numbers do not take into account the actual, excuse me, these numbers do not take into account employment effects in manufacturing and other industries that have benefited from lower electricity and feed stock prices. Additionally, the Nation's oil and gas industry provides significant revenue to both Federal and State governments.

The governments receive $85 million per day from the oil and natural gas industry while State and local governments receive millions more. An important component of the Nation's oil and gas industry is the offshore industry centered around the central and western Gulf of Mexico with some legacy production off California and Alaska. The Gulf of Mexico alone produces around 1.3 million barrels of oil per day and 3.6 billion cubic feet of natural gas.

Estimates of current employment due to the offshore oil and natural gas industry produced by Quest are around 375,000 total jobs of which around 100,000 are directly in the industry. Employment is centered around the Gulf Coast States with these States accounting for around 70 percent of total employment. But the effects are felt throughout the country. Additionally the industry is estimated to provide over nine billion a year of revenue to the Federal Government.

The contributions of the offshore oil and natural gas industry, in particular, are limited due to the fact that approximately 85 percent of acreage in the Federal offshore waters is inaccessible to offshore oil and natural gas development either through a lack of Federal lease sales or outright moratoriums. The only Federal OCS areas which are unrestricted for leasing are the central and western Gulf with 98 percent of the eastern Gulf, all the Atlantic OCS and the Pacific OCS inaccessible for new activity. Increasing the oil and natural gas industry's access to Federal waters would likely increase domestic energy production, contribute to greater employment and provide increased revenues to the Federal and State governments.

As an example of the possible impacts of increasing access to the U.S. OCS for oil and natural gas development I'll present a brief overview of a study recently completed by Quest Offshore on the possible impacts of opening the Atlantic OCS to offshore oil and natural gas activity.

Oil and natural gas development off the Atlantic Coast has been restricted since the 1980s with a lease sale canceled off the Coast of Virginia that was planned for 2011. No lease sales in the Atlantic OCS are currently scheduled. Although plans for seismic in the area have just been approved and discussions on limited leasing in the upcoming 5 year plan have taken place.

The Quest report completed in 2013 constructed a scenario of oil and gas development in the Atlantic OCS based on the resource potential of the area, geologic analogs and the full value chain of the oil and gas industry. The study found that if leasing in the Atlantic OCS began in 2018 with seismic in 2017 the annual capital investment and other spending would be projected to grow from nearly $7 billion a year in 2025 to nearly $20 billion a year in 2035. Cumulative capital investment and other spending from 2017 to 2035 was projected at about $195 billion.

Atlantic Coast OCS oil and gas activities could create nearly 80,000 jobs by 2025 of which nearly 45,000 would be in the Atlantic States. By 2035 total national employment due to the Atlantic OCS oil and gas production would reach about 280,000 jobs with 215,000 of these jobs in the Atlantic States. Combined State and Federal revenue from bonuses, rents and royalties were projected to reach about $645 million per year in 2025 with these revenues projected to grow to nearly $12.2 billion a year in 2035.

If a legislated State/Federal revenue sharing agreement was enacted the Atlantic States could see significant gains to their budgets. With a 37.5 percent revenue sharing agreement State revenue is projected to be about $250 million per year by 2025 with these revenues expected to grow to around $4.5 billion a year by 2035.

Important to note that no revenue sharing legislations in place in the Atlantic and also, you know, any caps or anything else that were enacted would affect that.

Additionally the report projected that the Atlantic OCS oil and gas development could produce about 1.35 million barrels of oil equivalent per day by 2035.

Under this scenario it's pretty clear that allowing access to the Atlantic OCS as well as other areas would cause significant increases in employment, government revenues as well as overall economic activity. Allowing access to the remainder of the 85 percent of the Federal OCS which is inaccessible would undoubtedly have similar effects.

Thank you.

[The prepared statement of Mr. Shafer follows:]

PREPARED STATEMENT OF SEAN SHAFER, CONSULTING MANAGER, QUEST OFFSHORE RESOURCES, INC., SUGAR LAND, TX

Good Morning Chairman Landrieu, Ranking Member Murkowski, and Members of the Committee, my name is Sean Shafer and I would like to thank you for the opportunity to testify before the committee.

The nation's oil and natural gas industry supports 9.8 million U.S. jobs and 8 percent of the U.S. economy. Approximately 2.6 million of the jobs are directly within the oil and gas industry. Due their on average higher paying nature, many jobs within the oil and gas industry tend to have larger effects on overall employment throughout the economy. Additionally, the oil and natural gas industry has been at the forefront of the nation's economic recovery, experiencing job growth at a significantly faster rate than the rest of the economy. From 2007 to 2012 oil and gas employment grew 40 percent compared to overall employments 1 percent growth, accounting for around 160 thousand of the total one million new jobs created in this period. These numbers do not take into account employment effects in manufacturing and other industries that have undoubtedly benefited from lower electricity and feedstock prices, driven by increased domestic production of oil and natural gas.

Additionally, the nation's oil and natural gas industry provides significant revenue to both the Federal and state governments. The Federal Government alone receives $85 million per day from the oil and natural gas industry while state and local governments also receive millions more.

An important component of the nation's oil and natural gas industry is the offshore industry, centered on the central and western Gulf of Mexico with some legacy activity off California and Alaska. The Gulf of Mexico alone produces around 1.3 million barrels of oil per day, and 3.6 billion cubic feet per day of natural gas. Estimates of current employment due to the offshore oil and natural gas industry produced by Quest are around 375 thousand total jobs, of which around 100 thousand jobs are directly in the industry. Employment is centered in the Gulf Coast states, with these states accounting for around 70 percent of employment, but the employment effects are felt throughout the country. Additionally, the offshore oil and natural gas industry is estimated to provide over $9 billion/year of revenue to the Federal Government.

The contributions of the offshore oil and natural gas industry in particular are limited due to the fact that approximately 85 percent of acreage in Federal offshore waters is inaccessible to offshore oil and natural gas development, either through a lack of Federal lease sales or outright moratoriums. The only Federal OCS areas with unrestricted leasing are the central and western Gulf of Mexico, with 98 percent of the Eastern Gulf of Mexico, all of the Atlantic OCS, and the Pacific OCS inaccessible for new activity. Increasing the oil and natural gas industry's access to US Federal waters would likely increase domestic energy production, contribute to greater employment, and provide increased revenues to the Federal and state governments.

As an example of the possible impacts of increasing access to the US OCS for oil and natural development I will present a brief overview of a study recently completed by Quest Offshore on the possible impacts of opening the Atlantic OCS to offshore oil and natural gas activity. Oil and gas development off the Atlantic coast has been restricted since the 1980s. A lease sale off the coast of Virginia was planned for 2011, but was subsequently canceled. No lease sales in the Atlantic Outer Continental Shelf (OCS) are currently scheduled although plans for seismic in the area have just been approved and discussions on limited leasing in the upcoming 5 year plan have taken place.

Quest's report completed in December 2013 constructed a scenario of oil and natural gas development in the Atlantic OCS, based on the resource potential of the area, geologic analogs, and the full value chain of oil and natural gas development and production. The study found that if leasing in the Atlantic OCS began in 2018 and seismic in 2017, annual capital investment and other spending would be projected to grow from nearly $7 billion per year in 2025 to nearly $20 billion per year in 2035. Cumulative capital investments and other spending from 2017 to 2035 were projected at about $195 billion.

Atlantic coast OCS oil and gas activities could create nearly 80 thousand jobs by 2025, of which nearly 40 thousand would be in the Atlantic coast states. By 2035, total national employment due to Atlantic OCS oil and gas exploration and production would reach nearly 280 thousand jobs, with 215 thousand of these jobs in Atlantic coast states.

Combined state and Federal revenues from bonuses, rents and royalties were projected to reach about $645 million per year in 2025, with these revenues projected to grow to nearly $12.2 billion per year in 2035.

If a legislated state / Federal revenue sharing agreement was enacted, the Atlantic coast states could see significant gains to their state budgets. With a 37.5 percent sharing agreement, state revenues were projected to be around $250 million per year by 2025, with these revenues expected to grow to over $4.5 billion per year by 2035. Due to a lack of current Atlantic revenue sharing legislation all projected state revenues would be subject to adjustment depending on any future legislation.

Additionally, the report projected that development of the Atlantic coast's offshore oil and natural gas reserves would lead to production of around 1.35 million barrels of oil equivalent per day by 2035.

Under the scenario laid out in the study it is clear that allowing access to the Atlantic OCS for oil and natural gas activities would have a significant effect on the economy, employment and government revenues. Allowing access to the remainder of the 85 percent of the Federal OCS which is currently inaccessible to offshore oil and natural gas development would undoubtedly have similar effects.

The CHAIR. Thank you, Mr. Shafer.
Dr. Nelson.

## STATEMENT OF LAURA NELSON, DIRECTOR OF THE UTAH GOVERNOR'S, OFFICE OF ENERGY DEVELOPMENT, SALT LAKE CITY, UT

Ms. NELSON. Thank you, Chairman Landrieu and Ranking Member Murkowski and members of the committee. I appreciate the opportunity to testify here today. My name is Laura Nelson and I am the Director of the Utah Office of Energy Development.

I'm going to focus this morning primarily on energy revenues and energy jobs. However, I think it's important to note that mining and agriculture are also critical natural resource sectors in Utah, as are our State and national parks. We leverage all of these natural resources to generate revenues and create jobs.

Unfortunately given our status as a public land State, Utah is not at liberty to chart its own course to determine how to best balance its development and conservation goals. Utah is willing and we've proven our ability to manage natural resources effectively. But we remain subject to arcane Federal regulatory processes that hinder our natural, environmentally responsible, economic growth.

I want to note that energy jobs in Utah account for 1.4 percent of the State's jobs. That's just under 18,000 jobs. But this is 2.6 percent of total wages in the State.

This correctly suggests that energy jobs are unusually high paying jobs. The average energy job in Utah pays about 190 percent of the State's median wage.

With respect to the State's energy revenues they flow a variety of sources, Federal mineral leases, severance taxes, royalties from school and institutional trust lands, property taxes, sales taxes, income tax and conservation tax. Of these the most significant are the property taxes and Federal mineral leases. They account for, combined in 2012, about 60 percent of the $577 million in energy revenue to the State.

Utah has benefited significantly from energy booms in recent decades. In today's boom which we're experiencing seems to have staying power. It's driven by market conditions as well as the technological revolution that has come in the form of new drilling and well stimulation technologies. We believe to the extent that we can access our resources, we can create sustained growth in the development and activity and the associated jobs and revenues while balancing the need for a proactive environmental management.

Unfortunately in a public lands State that is 70 percent federally owned, the ability to access and responsibly develop our natural resources is dramatically impeded by the abstruse environmental and species regulations. In addition to those regulations we've seen significant reductions in permits and other lease sales from the BLM over the last few years. During the previous administration's 8 years Utah saw an average of 300 thousand acres leased per year. In the current administration's first term that number was just over 85,000 acres. That means that annually the administration has leased less than 30 percent as much land as during the Bush Administration.

Despite that Utah has continued to see growth in its oil and gas industries.

In oil production we grew from 15 million barrels per year to over 35 million barrels per year. That growth is fueled largely by activities on State trust lands and private lands.

Now I've really focused here on conventional energy production but I also want to note that we have a nascent solar industry. The reason I focused on oil and gas production and conventional energy is it's 95 percent of our energy and revenue jobs. But we do see great potential for solar.

In the past year due to the 1978 Public Utilities Regulatory Policy Act we have seen significant solar development activity as market conditions have aligned with utility's obligations under this act. What we have seen is that 19 projects ranging in size from 2 to 80 megawatts have signed power purchase agreements with PacifiCorp. Of those solar projects not a single one is to be constructed on public land even though most of these are in the southwest portion of the State where 85 percent of the lands are under Federal control.

The indication is that even for the solar industry which seems to be supported by this administration doesn't really see Federal lands as an option for development.

I also want to mention that we have a large, untapped resource in oil shale and oil sands resources perhaps our largest resource. With 77 billion barrels of oil recoverable from oil shale and 15 barrels of oil recoverable from oil sands, these are perhaps Utah's most promising energy resources in terms of future revenue and job creation potential. The keen challenge is that unlike solar, oil shale and oil sands seems to have been designated as non preferred energy options.

The key for us is success—is access. The key to our success is access. The State's goal is to take back the reins, to the extent possible, so they can follow a resource development path that makes sense for Utah.

We have learned and we have demonstrated that conservation and economic development can go hand in hand. We believe that our partners in DC should support an increased role for the State in managing its resources.

Thank you so much for allowing us to testify here today. I look forward to answering any questions you have.

[The prepared statement of Ms. Nelson follows:]

PREPARED STATEMENT OF LAURA NELSON, DIRECTOR OF THE UTAH GOVERNOR'S OFFICE OF ENERGY DEVELOPMENT, SALT LAKE CITY, UT

This morning I will focus primarily on energy revenues and energy jobs; however, mining and agriculture are also critical natural resource sectors in Utah, as are our state and national parks. Utah leverages all its natural resources profoundly to generate revenue and create jobs. Unfortunately, given its status as a public lands state, Utah is not at liberty to chart its own course, to determine how best to balance its development and conservation goals. Utah is willing— and has proven itself able—to manage its natural resources effectively, but we remain subject to arcane Federal regulatory processes that hinder our natural, environmentally responsible economic growth.

In particular, energy jobs in Utah account for 1.4 percent of the state's jobs -just under 18,000 -but account for 2.6 percent of the state's total wages; correctly suggesting that energy jobs are unusually high-paying. The average energy job in Utah pays about 190 percent of the state's median wage.

With respect to the state's energy revenues, they flow through the following means: Federal mineral leases, severance taxes, royalties from the School and Institutional Trust Lands Administration permanent fund, property taxes, sales tax, income tax, and conservation tax. Of these, most significant are the property taxes and Federal Mineral Leases, which in 2012 made up over 60 percent of the $577 million in energy revenue to the state.

**Utah's Energy Revenue**

| | Gross Value ($M) | Property ($M) | Sales ($M) | Severance ($M) | Conservation Fee ($M) | SITLA ($M) | Federal Royalties ($M) | Income ($M) | Total Revenue ($M) |
|---|---|---|---|---|---|---|---|---|---|
| Oil and Gas | 3,871 | 57 | 9 | 66 | 6 | 59 | 148 | 33 | 379 |
| Coal | 626 | 4 | N/A | N/A | N/A | 10 | 18 | 7 | 39 |
| Solar | 1 | N/A | N/A | N/A | N/A | N/A | N/A | | 0 |
| Wind | 53 | 7 | N/A | N/A | N/A | N/A | N/A | 0 | 7 |
| Hydroelectric | 85 | | | | | | | | |
| Geothermal | 25 | | | | | | | | |
| Total Energy Dev. | 4,663 | 68 | 9 | 66 | 6 | 69 | 166 | 40 | 425 |
| Other Energy | N/A | 124 | | N/A | N/A | N/A | N/A | 28 | 152 |
| Total All Energy | 4,663 | 192 | 9 | 66 | 6 | 69 | 166 | 68 | 577 |

*Utah Office of Energy Development*

Utah has benefited from energy booms in recent decades, and today's boom seems certain to have staying power; because it is driven not only by market conditions, but also by a technological revolution that has come in the form of new drilling and well-stimulation techniques. We believe that to the extent that we can access our resources, we can create a sustained growth in development activity and in associated jobs and revenues, while balancing the need for proactive environmental management.

Unfortunately, in a public lands state that is 70 percent federally owned, the ability to access and responsibly develop our natural resources is dramatically impeded by abstruse environmental and species regulations. In addition to those regulations, we've seen a significant reduction in permits and/or lease sales from the BLM over the last few years. During the previous administration's 8 years at the helm, Utah saw an average of over 300,000 acres leased per year, and in the current administration's first term that number was just under 85,000 acres. That means that annually this administration's BLM has leased less than 30 percent as much land as during the Bush Administration in any given year.

**BLM Leasing Trends in Utah**

| Fiscal Year (Oct-Sept) | Competitive Leasing | | | | | |
|---|---|---|---|---|---|---|
| | Lands Nominated | | Lands Offered | | Lands Leased | |
| | Parcels | Total Acres | Parcels | Total Acres | Leases | Total Acres |
| 2000 | 504 | 700,378 | 316 | 481,959 | 122 | 165,499 |
| 2001 | 289 | 363,088 | 212 | 270,835 | 120 | 146,582 |
| 2002 | 365 | 531,538 | 152 | 188,609 | 75 | 92,650 |
| 2003 | 358 | 498,512 | 219 | 284,456 | 134 | 149,395 |
| 2004 | 785 | 1,106,101 | 502 | 784,098 | 377 | 563,652 |
| 2005 | 981 | 1,450,295 | 329 | 505,563 | 280 | 421,320 |
| 2006 | 1122 | 1,683,265 | 653 | 999,533 | 550 | 828,886 |
| 2007 | 901 | 1,286,813 | 390 | 556,625 | 294 | 386,014 |
| 2008 | 324 | 459,920 | 124 | 163,391 | 105 | 143,105 |
| 2009 | 729 | 934,112 | 308 | 413,443 | 229 | 299,895 |
| 2010 | 317 | 482,103 | 38 | 45,144 | 18 | 14,228 |
| 2011 | 208 | 365,592 | 17 | 23,114 | 5 | 2,958 |
| 2012 | 469 | 909,364 | 45 | 54,657 | 24 | 20,467 |

*Bureau of Land Management*

Remarkably, notwithstanding this trend Utah's growth in production has been steady. During the same 12 year period-2001–2012-Utah's oil production grew from 15 million barrels per year to over 35 million barrels per year. That growth is fueled largely by activities on state trust lands and private lands.

I have mostly been addressing conventional energy production, because in Utah that drives approximately 95 percent of energy revenue and jobs. However when we're talking about development activities favoring private and state lands, Utah's still-nascent solar industry is particularly telling. Over the past twelve months market conditions have aligned with utilities' obligations under the 1978 Public Utilities Regulatory Policy act to generate significant solar development activity, and this has occurred without a Renewable Portfolio Standard. Indeed, during that time 19 projects ranging in size from 2 to 80 megawatts have signed power purchase contracts with PacifiCorp.

Of those solar projects, not a single one is to be constructed on Federal land. And these projects are proposed for the southwest portion of the state, an area where more like 85 percent of lands are under Federal control. The indication is that even the solar development community, an industry sector that is unequivocally endorsed by the Obama administration, has determined that developing projects on Federal land in Utah is simply a non-starter. And this is true regardless of the federally designated "Solar Energy Zones."

*In 2013, Utah produced:*

- 35 million barrels of oil;
- 471 million MCF of natural gas; and
- 17 million tons of coal.

Solar is an exciting opportunity poised for explosive growth. However, capacity limitations, land requirements, and infrastructure constraints will limit solar's contribution to Utah's overall energy jobs and revenue picture. Our foundational resources are oil, gas, and coal. Utah is 11th among states in oil production, 9th among states in natural gas production, and 15th among states in coal production. Our as-yet-untapped oil shale and oil sands resources are by far the largest resources in the country, with 77 billion barrels of oil recoverable from oil shale, and 15 billion barrels of oil recoverable from oil sands. These are perhaps Utah's most promising energy resources in terms of future revenue and job creation potential. The numbers are staggering.

The keen challenge is that, unlike solar, oil shale and oil sands seem to have been designated as "non-preferred" energy option. The Department of the Interior appears to be restricting commercial demonstration of these promising opportunities through draconian restrictions in leasing justified by the preconceived notion that oil sands and oil shale technologies are not yet commercially viable. Additionally, perennial threats of new listings under the Endangered Species Act are further restricting the commercial demonstration of these promising resources.

The State of Utah's goal is to take back the reigns, to the extent possible, so that it can follow a resource development path that makes sense for Utahns. As mentioned earlier, Utahns and their elected leaders fully value the economic and social values underpinned by the state's pristine natural environment. The state's diverse beauty attracts tourism, outdoor recreation, the film industry, and many other sectors that are essential to the state economy. It also provides multiple benefits to Utahns. It is therefore in the state's interest to preserve Utah's natural environment while at the same time responsibly developing its natural resources. Utahns have learned—and demonstrated—that conservation and economic development can go hand in hand, and it's time for our partners in Washington D.C. to support an increased role for the state in managing its resources. This will allow Utah's policymakers, its regulators, its development community and other stakeholders to find the right balance for Utah's energy and natural resource opportunities.

**Percentage of Property Tax From Energy Development**

| County | Electric Power | Pipeline & Gas Utilities | Oil & Gas Extraction | Coal Mines | Energy-Related Total | % County Total |
|---|---|---|---|---|---|---|
| Beaver | 4,005,401 | 781,190 | - | - | 4,786,591 | 47% |
| Carbon | 1,212,365 | 929,868 | 5,875,469 | 2,013,815 | 10,031,517 | 44% |
| Daggett | 18,078 | 910,660 | 79,558 | | 1,008,296 | 45% |
| Duchesne | 513,882 | 435,967 | 8,755,478 | - | 9,705,327 | 41% |
| Emery | 18,294,819 | 55,046 | 878,589 | 826,773 | 20,055,227 | 81% |
| Juab | 2,940,010 | 779,865 | - | 16,380 | 3,736,255 | 37% |
| Millard | 12,026,872 | 1,515,244 | - | - | 13,542,116 | 62% |
| San Juan | 786,959 | 728,963 | 4,983,254 | - | 6,499,176 | 47% |
| Sevier | 543,802 | 66,628 | 2,034,055 | 1,282,057 | 3,926,542 | 29% |
| Uintah | 1,716,184 | 1,978,536 | 24,128,270 | 64 | 27,823,054 | 57% |
| Statewide | 76,285,872 | 35,031,612 | 48,652,269 | 4,307,474 | 164,277,227 | 7% |

The CHAIR. Thank you very much, Doctor.
Mr. Taylor.

## STATEMENT OF DUANE TAYLOR, DIRECTOR, FEDERAL AFFAIRS, MOTORCYCLE INDUSTRY COUNCIL, ARLINGTON, VA

Mr. TAYLOR. Thank you.

Chairman Landrieu, Ranking Member Murkowski and distinguished members of the committee, thank you for the opportunity to testify about the positive economic impact of responsible off highway vehicle recreation. I am Duane Taylor, Director of Federal Affairs for the Motorcycle Industry Council, Specialty Vehicle Institute of America and the Recreational Off Highway Vehicle Association.

MIC, SVIA and ROHVA are the trade associations that represent the power sports industry including the manufacturers of on and off highway motorcycles, all terrain vehicles and recreational off highway vehicles which are also known as side by sides.

The positive economic impact of recreation is well established. The just released Interior Economic Report for 2013 recognizes the important role recreation plays on DOI lands noting about recreation.

In Fiscal Year 2013 Interior's lands hosted an estimated 407 million visits.

For fiscal year 2013 value added provided by visitation to Interior sites was estimated to be $25 billion. Economic output was estimated to be $41 billion.

About 355,000 jobs were supported.

The Forest Service reports similar findings in its National Visitor Use Monitoring Results.

When it says, visits to National Forest lands are an important contribution to the economic vitality of rural communities.

Spending by recreation visitors in areas surrounding national forests amounted to nearly $11 billion.

Visitors who live more than 50 miles from the forest account for a bulk of these contributions. They spend about $5 billion annually.

As visitor spending ripples through the U.S. economy it contributes a little more than $13 billion to the GDP and sustains about 190,000 full and part time jobs."

The associations I represent recently joined with partners including the Outdoor Industry Association, the Western Governors' Association, to produce a report which also highlights the size and scope of the economic impact of recreation, finding that overall outdoor recreation generated $646 billion in national sales and services in 2011. This figure is far greater than—and supported 6.1 million jobs which is far greater than for example, the pharmaceutical and motor vehicle and parts industries.

Clearly recreation is big business. We have known this for quite some time. What we in the OHV communities have known for quite some time, but had never been studied nationally is that motorized recreation is a massive component of the revenues generated through outdoor recreation.

The economic impact of outdoor recreation to which I referred found that approximately $257 billion or nearly 40 percent of the total $646 billion in economic impact is derived from motorized recreation.

As I mentioned we in the industry and the broader OHV community expected these results as we know firsthand the irreplaceable, positive, economic impact motorized recreation opportunities have had in many rural areas. I'm thinking of small towns and communities near the Paiute ATV trail in Utah or surrounding the Hatfield-McCoy Trails in West Virginia or all over the State of Colorado as existing economic impact studies have already found that motorized recreation can revitalize and/or sustain rural economies that have been hard hit by the recession.

It is important to highlight the value of motorized recreation so that land managers and other decisionmakers can make informed decisions about how best to manage public lands. While it is clear that OHV recreation isn't appropriate everywhere, properly managed and sustainable motorized recreation opportunities can demonstrably provide a dramatic, positive, economic boost to small towns and businesses across the Nation.

While OHV enthusiasts are encouraging Interior, Forest Service and other officials to maintain or expand sustainable motorized recreation through any manner of planning processes at the local level, we feel it is important that Congress, as well as the Administration, hear the positive economic message about motorized recreation as you make decisions about the designations of wilderness, national monuments and other special designations of public lands.

We fully understand that there are spectacular and pristine areas of public lands that deserve special designation and should be set aside for limited uses. However, we are concerned that specially designating massive swaths of public lands is the wrong way forward. These enormous and inappropriate designations may either completely rule out or lead to the restriction or elimination of motorized recreation as well as other multiple use activities where they would otherwise be appropriate and could benefit rural economies.

We encourage each of you to carefully consider land use legislation and the input of all relevant, local stakeholders to ensure that managed, sustainable, motorized recreation is maintained or expanded, where appropriate, so that the full economic impact of recreation can be realized.

Also, last, I would be remiss if I didn't thank Senator Murkowski for introducing S. 2068. We look forward to working with you on this legislation.

Thank you.

[The prepared statement of Mr. Taylor follows:]

PREPARED STATEMENT OF DUANE TAYLOR, DIRECTOR, FEDERAL AFFAIRS MOTORCYCLE INDUSTRY COUNCIL, ARLINGTON, VA

Chairman Landrieu, Ranking Member Murkowski and distinguished Members of the Committee -thank you for the opportunity to testify about the positive economic impact of responsible off-highway vehicle recreation. I am Duane Taylor, Director, Federal Affairs for the Motorcycle Industry Council (MIC), Specialty Vehicle Institute of America (SVIA) and the Recreational Off-Highway Vehicle Association (ROHVA). MIC, SVIA and ROHVA are the trade associations that represent the powersports industry including the manufacturers of on and off-highway motorcycles, all-terrain vehicles and recreational off-highway vehicles -also known as side-by-sides.

The positive economic impact of recreation is well established. The just-released DOI economic report for fiscal year 2013 recognizes the important role recreation plays on DOI lands noting about recreation:

In fiscal year 2013, Interior's lands hosted an estimated 407 million visits. For fiscal year 2013, value added provided by visitation to Interior sites was estimated to be $25 billion, economic output was estimated to be $41 billion and about 355,000 jobs were supported.

The Forest Service reports similar findings in its National Visitor Use Monitoring Results:

Visits to National Forest lands are an important contribution to the economic vitality of rural communities. Spending by recreation visitors in areas surrounding National Forests amounted to nearly $11 billion. Visitors who live more than 50 miles from the forest account for the bulk of these contributions; they spend about $5 billion annually. As visitor spending ripples through the US economy, it contributes a little more than $13 billion to GDP, and sustains about 190,000 full and part time jobs.

The associations I represent recently joined with partners including the Outdoor Industry Association and the Western Governors' Association to produce a report which also highlights the size and scope of the economic impact of recreation, finding that overall outdoor recreation generated $646 billion in national sales and services in 2011 and supported 6.1 million jobs which is far greater than, for example, the pharmaceutical and motor vehicle and parts industries.

Clearly recreation is big business -we have known this for quite some time. What we in the OHV community have known for quite some time, but that had never been studied nationally, is that motorized recreation is a massive component of the revenues generated through outdoor recreation. The Economic Impact of Outdoor Recreation, to which I referred found that that approximately $257 billion or nearly 40 percent of the total $646 billion in economic impact is derived from motorized recreation.

As I mentioned, we in the industry and the broader OHV community expected these results as we know first-hand the irreplaceable positive economic impact motorized recreation opportunities have had in many rural areas. I am thinking of small towns and communities near the Paiute ATV trail in Utah, or surrounding the Hatfield-McCoy Trails in West Virginia, or all over the state of Colorado as existing economic impact studies have already found that motorized recreation can revitalize and/or sustain rural economies that have been hard hit by the recession.

It is important to highlight the value of motorized recreation so that land managers and other decisionmakers can make informed decisions about how best to manage public lands. While it is clear that OHV recreation isn't appropriate everywhere, properly managed and sustainable motorized recreation opportunities can demonstrably provide a dramatic positive economic boost to small towns and businesses across the Nation.

While OHV enthusiasts are encouraging DOI, Forest Service and other officials to maintain or expand sustainable motorized recreation through any manner of planning processes at the local level we feel it is important that Congress, and the Administration as well, hear the positive economic message about motorized recreation as you make decisions about the designation of wilderness, National Monuments and other special designations of public lands.

We fully understand that there are spectacular and pristine areas of public lands that deserve special designation and should be set aside for limited uses; however, we are concerned that specially designating massive swaths of public lands is the wrong way forward. These enormous and inappropriate designations may either completely rule out, or lead to the restriction or elimination of motorized recreation as well as other multiple use activities where they would otherwise be appropriate and could benefit rural economies.

We encourage each of you to carefully consider land use legislation and the input of all relevant local stakeholders to ensure that managed, sustainable motorized recreation is maintained or expanded where appropriate so that the full economic impact of recreation can be realized.

Thank you.

The CHAIR. Thank you all for that excellent testimony.

Let me start, Ms. Randolph, with you and thank you for your long standing leadership, not just in our State, but around the country as a leader for coastal revenue sharing.

I have two questions for you.

One, you testified that Port Fourchon which is in your parish, Port Fourchon helps to generate nearly nine billion a year for the Federal Treasury. Is that correct and can you give 30 seconds about if this port wasn't there how would this money get out of the Gulf of Mexico?

Ms. RANDOLPH. Thank you, Senator.

Yes, Port Fourchon is the geographic location for deep water drilling. Therefore because of its close proximity to that operation it essentially cuts down time and cuts down costs to get to that energy production. In doing so is able to produce energy for this Nation at a lower cost and second, produce money for the Federal Treasury in the form of royalties and severance taxes.

So, Port Fourchon is the significant port as far as generating Federal moneys.

The CHAIR. It's not the only energy port, but it is designated, not by the Federal Government, but by the industry itself as, sort of, the center of deep water operations which is responsible for a great portion of this nine billion.

You said there's a road, LA 1. That is a highway, the only highway that leads to Port Fourchon. You testified that it would only cost $315 million to complete if we did that over 5 years, about $60 million a year for 5 years.

Over that same period of time the Gulf will generate for the Federal Treasury $45 billion. Nine times 5 is $45 billion.

Do you see any reason that the Federal Government couldn't pick up a greater portion of the building of the only highway to Port Fourchon that generates that extraordinary amount of money for the country?

Ms. RANDOLPH. First let me acknowledge your leadership in providing some of the funds that have brought us to this point.

But second, the answer is no. We do see certainly sufficient money to pay for this highway, to ensure its continued—the port's continued operation which would continue the flow of money to the Federal Treasury.

The CHAIR. Describe, real quickly, is this a 4 lane highway or a 6 lane highway? What is this highway look like, its original form?

Ms. RANDOLPH. It's a 2 lane.

The CHAIR. Is it elevated at all or is it at or below sea level?

Ms. RANDOLPH. The portion that is unimproved is below sea level and so anytime——

The CHAIR. Does that make any sense to you to have a 2 lane highway below sea level connecting America which is a great energy super power with a resource that generates $9 billion a year for the Federal Treasury?

Ms. RANDOLPH. No, Senator, it does not. We also tolled this road in order to repay the loan.

The CHAIR. So the people that live there that use it the most have to pay for the whole country to generate the $9 billion for the Nation?

Ms. RANDOLPH. That's correct, Senator.

The CHAIR. Yed.

Let me ask you, Mr. Webster.

Your call for access, I think, is really important for the sportsmen. That's very important to the culture and history of Louisiana
and Alaska. Of course, you're looking at the 2 powerful sportsmen
States and others but—and sportswomen States, I should say.

But the access that you seek, is there any conflict with the access
that Mr. Taylor seeks with the motorized sport access as opposed
to the traditional hunting and fishing or have your organizations
figured out a way to work together or is there any conflict? I'm
going to ask both of you.

Mr. WEBSTER. I mean, it's a great question. The access that I referred to most specifically is access to public lands. There's actually
a lot of public lands that you can't even get to because they're landlocked. There's basically, significant areas of public land that you
just can't even get to unless you maybe fly in or something like
that.

So having those programs like making public lands public or the
Hunt Act would actually, you know, provide money to work with
landowners.

The CHAIR. Making public lands actually public.

Mr. WEBSTER. Making public lands actually public.

I think in terms of once you get onto those forests, you know, we
support multiple use management which means that motorized access is clearly an important component of uses on public lands.
There's also areas that have priority fish and wildlife habitats
where, you know, there needs to be conservation in place to make
sure that those habitats produce a lot of wildlife. That is done at
the local level through the local land use planning.

I think we probably both agree that, you know, we look at local
land use plans there may be some things in there that we'd do a
little differently. But that's—but I think conceptually we agree.

The CHAIR. Conceptually it can be worked out at the local level
usually.

Mr. WEBSTER. Yes.

The CHAIR. Mr. Taylor, real quick, 30 seconds.

Mr. TAYLOR. Sure, yes. I would pretty much agree with what he
said. Say that there is a, you know, pretty significant amount of
overlap between the people who buy our member's products and
the people who go hunt and fish. In fact, a lot of hunters use ATVs
and ROVs for those purposes.

There's obviously a great opportunity for us and other organizations to work together. We'd be happy to do that.

The CHAIR. Including it's not just the off road vehicles, but it's
the recreational vehicles, the RVs, the camping industry is a huge
industry in our State. In fact, Angus King just told me he's going
on a camping trip with his RV and wants to come down to visit in
Louisiana. So we'll look forward to hosting him, the Senator from
Maine.

Senator Murkowski.

Senator MURKOWSKI. Thank you, Madame Chairman.

As we're talking about motorized vehicles I had an opportunity
to go to the southern border on Friday, out to McAllen, Texas. Very
clear impressions there, that as we deal with border enforcement
issues part of our reality in being hamstrung in our ability to enforce is that we have public lands along that border that are held

by the Department of Interior in refuge and wilderness status. We can't get access to a road, to a trail for an ATV so our customs and border patrol agents can patrol that.

We're not asking for a major highway around there, but I know that this hearing is designed to look specifically at how we derive revenues. We also need to think about national security issues and how we enforce our own laws when you juxtapose that with other priorities within the Federal agencies. It's something that I'm working on and I would hope that the Committee would have an opportunity to look at just that.

I wanted to comment, Dr. Nelson, on some of the points that you raised and the fact that in Utah you are, you're, actually working to expand your access in certain areas despite the Federal policies. What I've heard from just about every one of you is that whether it's in oil and gas or whether it's what we're doing for multiple use and recreation—motorized vehicles, we're, kind of, doing it in spite of some of the hurdles that are put in place from a Federal perspective.

The example again of not being able to site solar facilities on our public lands, it just seems so inconsistent with this message from this Administration that we want to move toward renewables. Here's Utah, a perfect example.

You have oil and gas resources.

You've got the potential for renewable.

It's the Federal policies that are limited your ability to access any of them.

I—the term that you used, Dr. Nelson, non-preferred energy options, is one that, I think, we need to be paying attention to. You can't say we have an all of the above energy policy while at the same time say that some of these are not exactly preferred. So I think it is important that our States do what they can to, as you say, take back the reins.

Easier said than done, but these are issues that, I think, that we need to address.

The Director is still in the room with us here, Madame Chairman. I'm going to be submitting a couple other questions to him for the record. But one that I would like him to look into is according to honors statistics.

Back in 2003 the reported revenue from Alaska was $97.7 million. Just 10 years later in 2013 it was down to $33.6 million and this includes rents, royalties, bids, etcetera. So I'm going to be asking him to outline for me what he thinks explains this trend and whether or not it is reversible.

Senator MURKOWSKI. I think the question that I will leave Mr. Pearce with is one that relates to management of our timber resources in Alaska. As you may know the Governor in the State has appointed a State timber task force to come up with ideas as to how we can increase timber production. One of the recommendations from that task force was to create a 2 million acre State forest out of our current national forest system lands.

So the question to you is whether or not the National Forest Coalition and the Schools Coalition would support States managing some of our Federal lands on a pilot project basis to test the effectiveness of State management.

Is that something that the coalition has looked into and would be supportive of?

Mr. PEARCE. Absolutely. In fact there's a similar discussion at the—in Idaho. As you know, we have two and a half million acres of State trust land in our State which actually goes to counties, schools and at different levels. So absolutely we would support that.

Senator MURKOWSKI. Good. Good to hear that.

Mr. PEARCE. Be willing to help with that.

Senator MURKOWSKI. Great.

Then the last question here and this is to you, Mr. Shafer.

You have referred to the revenues that we see coming from offshore, but you also refer to the cancellation of the Atlantic lease sale back in 2011, lack of a current schedule. What does this lack of certainty going forward do to the prospects, not only for oil and gas revenues but just to the economy there in general?

Can you speak to that very quickly?

Mr. SHAFER. Yes, absolutely.

I mean, I think at this point the lack of certainty around, specifically, the Atlantic really is probably going to prevent any serious activity from operators. Within the last few days they've approved some seismic, you know, initial planning for seismic in the area. But without the prospect of actually saying, well in 3 years or 4 years or 5 years, we're going to be able to lease that area.

It really wouldn't make a lot of sense for operators, in my opinion, to go out and spend, you know, hundreds of millions of dollars to shoot those seismic studies without the prospect of actually being able to lease the lands in the future, so.

Senator MURKOWSKI. OK.

Thank you, Madame Chairman.

The CHAIR. Thank you.

We're joined by Senator Sanders for a round of questioning. I'll get to the Senator in just 1 second.

Mr. Pearce, I want to ask you this question about PILT, payment in lieu of taxes, as well as rural schools. It's a very important issue to many members of this committee. Louisiana doesn't benefit as much as some of the western States.

But as you can see on this chart up here this issue of Federal land and use of Federal land is really, it's almost a story of 2 different stories depending on whether you're an eastern State or a western State. Those of us in the middle are literally, in the middle.

There are, it looks like, 10 States that have more than 25 percent of their land owned by the Federal Government with the highest being Nevada at 81 percent, Utah at 66 and Alaska at only 61. I've been thinking it was much higher, but 61 is high. But Nevada is 81. Washington State is at 28 and then Hawaii is at 20 percent which would be interesting.

Then there are 10 or 12 States that have less than 2 percent of their land federally owned, Texas, Massachusetts, Maine, Rhode Island, New York, Kansas, Connecticut.

So it really is a tale of almost two countries, the way we treat Federal land and how we use it. They are very different perspectives based on whether you're in a State with 1 percent of Federal land or whether you're in the State of Nevada with 81 percent Federal land. You could see things very differently.

Our committee is really trying to find a way to unite the country over some of these issues. So we have quite a job ahead of us.

Let me ask you quickly and I'll get to Senator Sanders.

Tell me about rural schools.

Some members are very, very supportive of maintaining a more permanent source of funding, others, the ranking member said this in her opening statement. She supports it as a temporary bridge to getting back to timber sales. She'd rather cut timber and use it for the benefit of everyone rather than to watch it burn. We have a graph that's pretty dramatic about how much land is being burned.

You can't do anything with burned timber. Nobody can make a whole lot of money on it.

So what are your—what is NACo saying and the Westerners about rural schools? Do you want to see it permanent? Do you believe it should be temporary? Should we match it with some sort of increase in timber production or what is your ideal, you know, if you had to say, what is your ideal position on rural schools?

Mr. PEARCE. The folks that sit on my board that talk about this issue and especially the county, the schools, excuse me, and States where the money goes directly to the school. As you may know, many States, the money is actually—goes to the State and is used as part of an offset to their basic education.

So Washington schools receive a portion directly. California schools they get it totally.

We would like to see a return to at least more revenue production within those counties where the schools are located mainly because, as you look at SRS, and you look at the last 20 years without guarantee money and SRS, there's been a reduction over that period of time so folks are hanging on.

How much is the reduction going to be next year?

How much is the reduction going to be the year after?

The CHAIR. So they need a permanent—what they need is consistency.

Mr. PEARCE. Absolutely.

The CHAIR. Something they can plan for. The money, if it's the same rural schools, it should actually go to schools, not to the slush fund or general fund of States. It should actually work its way to schools.

If it is going to be made permanent or more reliable then you also would testify that you'd like to see timber harvest increased as well. Is that——

Mr. PEARCE. We believe timber harvest, sustainable timber harvest, sustainable forestry, is an absolute must in the West otherwise we are just going to burn it all up. We certainly are doing that now.

In my State that I come from you have the Wenatchee fire which is 109 square miles currently, 109 square miles. You had the forest fire last year in the Tehama County in California. It was 400 square miles.

I don't think people actually think in those terms. Often we talk about acres and folks aren't really used to acres unless you're a farmer or rancher. But when you talk about 400 square mile fires you realize how big that is.

Yes, we have to have forest management, no matter what, in order to manage this precious resource that we have. Timber harvest certainly is going to be part of that.

The CHAIR. Thank you.

Senator Sanders.

Senator SANDERS. Thank you, Madame Chair. I apologize for not having been here earlier. I thank the panelists for being with us.

I must say that this is a very interesting hearing because we talk about leveraging America's resources as a revenue generator and a job creator. We talk about how we might increase the production with the extraction of fossil fuel on Federal lands. Yet the most important issue facing our planet is not being discussed. That is whether or not we really do want to extract more fossil fuels from Federal lands or any other lands.

Mr. Pearce, a moment ago just made reference to the terrible forest fires we've seen in California and elsewhere. My understanding is that the forest fires of today are more severe, more frequent than they've ever been before. What I think the scientific community will tell you is, yes, that has a lot to do with climate change and the warming of the planet. Here we are talking about how we produce more carbon dioxide to warm the planet even more.

I think, Madame Chair, the President has asked for over $600 million to fight forest fires in the West. Then on and on it goes. So when we talk about revenue I think it's appropriate also to be talking about the fact that if we do not move away from fossil fuels and transform our energy system away from oil and coal and gas to sustainable energy and energy efficiency, the truth is that while, yes, I know extraction of fossil fuels will create jobs, will provide revenue.

But in the long run if we are creating a planetary crisis which will cost us hundreds and hundreds of billions of dollars and make the planet uninhabitable. I think we have to refocus how we think about this issue.

Madame Chair, I would just, for the record, mention that—and again when we talk about extreme weather nobody, you know, says that this event whether it was Katrina in your State or Irene in my State, is directly caused by global warming. But what the scientific community does tell us is that we are more likely, we are more likely, to see these types of events. There have always been forest fires. But the extent of forest fires today and the frequency of them, clearly, has a lot to do with the warming of the planet and the drying of the forests and so forth.

So I just would, for the record, like to point out when we talk about revenue, when we talk about money, extreme storms continue to cost us billions of dollars each year. According to a White House report released last fall, the U.S. has had 144 climate related storms that each cost a billion dollars or more since 1980. Combined these disasters have cost more than a trillion dollars.

In other words, taxpayers are spending huge sums of money. The estimate is that's only going to go up in order to fight the impact of climate change. In terms of forest fires, in terms of storms, in terms of floods, in terms of droughts, etcetera. NOAA reports that the super storm Sandy caused $65 billion in damage.

How many more super storms Sandy are we going to see unless we get a handle and reverse on climate change or reverse carbon emissions?

According to a report published in the Journal of Nature, flood damage in 136 of the world's largest coastal cities could start at a trillion dollars each year by 2050 because of climate change combined with rapid population increases. These trends are only escalating.

Frank Maddock, of the Reinsurance Association of America, Madame Chair, not noted as one of the more progressive organizations in the world citing the Munich Reinsurance Agency noted, "Globally climate change alone will increase worldwide losses for reinsurance companies by 100 percent by the end of the 21st century."

So I say, respectfully, and I, you know, very much appreciate all of the panelists for being here. But Madame Chair, it is just not good enough for us to continue to talk about some of the positive aspects of the production of fossil fuel. I know that there are. I know it creates jobs. I know it increases revenue. We all know that.

But we have to look at the broad picture and understand that if we don't transform our energy system and move away. I know it's not going to happen tomorrow, but start moving away aggressively from fossil fuel to energy efficiency. We talk about energy efficiency. We create substantial numbers of jobs weatherizing older homes in this country, getting our transportation system much more efficient.

When we talk about sustainable energy, solar. We're growing a whole lot of jobs in the solar energy, many of them good paying jobs. Wind. Geothermal. Biomass. Etcetera.

So, Madame Chair, I appreciate very much the testimony of our witnesses. I don't mean to be antagonistic. You're doing your jobs.

But I do believe that if we're going to say this planet and make it habitable for our kids and our grandchildren, we have to rethink some of the basic premises that we've been discussing today.

I thank you for the time, Madame Chair.

The CHAIR. Thank you, Senator Sanders, for that important perspective.

But I would note that, you know, as noticed in the hearing, this is much broader than oil and gas. It's about all resources on Federal lands, all income to Federal lands including recreation, including alternative energy sources, including solar, including sportsmen and non-energy related revenues.

What we have determined which is very interesting is that the total amount of revenues that come into the State from all these sources, I mean to the Federal Government, is equivalent to, well, since 1982, 1985, is $250 billion which is—sounds like a lot of money. It is. But it is only 1 year of corporate income tax receipts.

So from 1985 every dollar that the Federal Government has brought in in the management of its resources, all, timber, oil, gas, solar, minerals, recreation, hunting, fishing, etcetera. We're leaving out a little bit of the timber revenue because that's done in a different department, is $242 billion. In 1 year the corporations of America pay that in tax.

So in one hand, it's a lot of money. We have to be careful about how we spend it.

On the other hand you could argue that the environment is really getting short changed because we're not spending nearly enough of that to do coastal restoration, sustainable living, at least along the coast, using the benefit of the local advisory committees for smart land use.

Then Dr. Nelson, Senator, made a very good point. Would you restate that while the Senator is here, about the lack of solar on public land. If we should be moving to solar what is happening in Utah and what did you testify as to what's not happening on public land for solar?

Mr. NELSON. Thank you for that question.

You know, Utah really supports all types of energy development whether—and we have opportunities for all of it. We have geothermal. We have wind. We have solar. We have oil and gas. We have coal. Of course, we have the unconventional resources of oil shale and oil sands.

Solar, in particular, which I mentioned, as a nascent industry which we've really seen coming on board in the last year, really due in large part to market conditions plus the interest of the utilities aligning under the public utilities, PURPA, Public Utilities Regulatory Policy Act of 1978 has allowed this opportunity for these resources to develop.

We also, in Utah, have an extensive allocation of land that has been determined on federally managed land as a solar development zone. We, in the last, I want to say about a year, have had approximately 19 solar projects that have signed contracts with PacifiCorp, with the utility. None of those projects are located on federally managed lands. They are all either on private lands or State lands.

The reason is because the process of accessing the federally managed lands, even in the context of a defined renewable energy development zone, including solar energy development zone, the process is just too lengthy to realize the market benefits of developing.

Senator SANDERS. Madame Chair, I mean, I think Dr. Nelson makes a good and fair point.

Mr. NELSON. Yes.

Senator SANDERS. Something that we should examine. I guess I will conclude by saying I'm not a believer in all of the above. I know it's a catchy bumper sticker statement.

If some of all of the above is destroying our planet I think we have to limit what we are talking about. As I said before, I do need—I do believe that now is the time to transform our energy system.

I think Dr. Nelson is right. We've got to make it easier for people to develop solar projects, wind projects, geothermal, biomass, etcetera.

The CHAIR. On public lands.

Senator SANDERS. On public lands.

The CHAIR. Yes.

Senator SANDERS. So with that, Madame Chair, I thank you.

The CHAIR. Thank you.

Senator SANDERS. I thank the panel.

The CHAIR. Thank you all very much.

Let me ask one more question. Would you put up the Land and Water Conservation Fund because I've been a champion of funding the Land and Water Conservation Fund since I got here almost 20 years ago. It was created in 1965.

For the record of this committee, I want it to be noted that only in 2 years since 1985 or 2 years actually since the history of the program. It's not on here, but we went back and looked, since it was created in 1965.

So somebody help me with my math. That's more than 40 years, is almost 50 years. It will be fifty years this year or next year.

It has only been funded, fully funded, to the authorization level twice. So think about this. You should ask a question. Is this a success or a failure?

The creators wanted to take a portion, like a conservation royalty which makes a lot of sense from a stewardship position, from a leadership position, from are you being, the question. Are you being a good steward, if God was asking, you know, are you being a good steward?

When they created this I think they thought that the Federal Government would be willing to set aside just a few million dollars, one billion a year, $900 million a year, as a portion to give back to the environment, broadly speaking in many ways. State grants to do a broad range of things, to protect the environment and to promote, I guess economic development, etcetera. Recreation was a big part of this early finding for this group that created it.

It was actually based on a lot of local recreation needs of kids that live in places that they don't really ever see trees really. They don't see lakes. They can't access them unlike places in Louisiana where we take that for granted. There are millions and millions of children that have never, ever seen a lake, less alone had a chance to swim in one.

So this was created to help the public access public lands and to use the public lands for their benefit, revenue creating, job generating and pleasure and enjoyment. It's only been funded 2 years out of 50. So at the 50th anniversary I think we need to give it a good old try. You know? Let's try again to see if we can get this right.

That's going to be one of the goals in the piece of legislation that this committee puts forward is full funding for Land and Water Conservation and how the full funding will be $900 million. How it's allocated and to where it goes? It's going to be an interesting debate. How much of that is directed by Federal agencies and how much of it is directed at the State and county and local level for the benefit of the people actually on the ground in places so divergent as Utah, Vermont, Louisiana, Texas, California, Alaska.

So that is just a, I think, a really important touchstone that I wanted to get on the record before we conclude.

I'm going to give you all each, you know, 20 seconds to finish up something that you didn't get to say that you really feel like you want to get on this record. The record will stay open for 2 additional weeks.

But I think with the 50 year anniversary of the Land and Water Conservation Fund, the greatest destruction of land happening off the coast of Louisiana, the erosion of the land, almost a destruction of an internationally beloved city of New Orleans. This is a time to really review how, where these revenues are being generated. How they're being generated and how they should be disbursed for the benefit of the Nation, the taxpayer, the environment, to generate jobs, economic prosperity and to be good stewards of the land, air and water that we've all charged, we've all been charged to be.

Ms. Randolph, President Randolph, your concluding remarks?

Ms. RANDOLPH. Senator, you assisted us in forming Parishes Against Coastal Erosion because you saw that numbers would help us tell people about our cause and why—what we needed to do. We took that role and translated and discovered the National Association of Counties and learned that others throughout this country have natural resources which generates funding for the Federal Government. But have problems also with how they are allocated. How they're harvested. How they're mined. Every natural resource out there.

So we've learned that through this association we are going to continue to educate our community members, our State leaders and make this one of our major causes is ensure that these natural resources are—and the end product, the revenues generated by them are allocated back to those who feel the impact of them and back to those who enjoy their resources as well.

So thank you for this.

The CHAIR. Thank you very much.

Mr. Pearce.

Mr. PEARCE. Yes, we fully support the full funding of LWCF. We think that that it has to go back to some of the original intensions. Monies to the States, to the counties, to the State parks, so on which has been lost along the way to some extent.

Clearly we think that there's a connection between LWCF and potentially funding PILT and SRS. We do believe that SRS needs to be fully funded so that these schools and these counties continue to get the services that they need to give, as I discussed in my testimony. But clearly we need to find appropriate ways to manage those forests that we have.

Thank you.

The CHAIR. Thank you.

Mr. Webster.

Mr. WEBSTER. Madame Chairwoman, in addition to, you know, restating our full support for the Land and Water Conservation Fund, I did want to bring up one of the issues that ties a lot of things we've been discussing today which is wildfire disaster funding. As a result of significantly increased costs in fighting wildfires the U.S. Forest Service's budget has basically been hammered when it comes to doing other things like managing the forest and actually reducing fuel loads to reduce the potential for future fires.

The Wildfire Disaster Funding Act, S. 1875, you know, would take the most extreme fires and create an emergency account for those 1 percent of fires. So when we did reach those levels that money would come out of a separate account and help ensure that the Forest Service could continue to do its job which is really important when it comes to managing wildlife habitat, but also preventing, you know, fire.

The CHAIR. Thank you for raising that. That was a subject of last week's hearing. I was happy to conduct a hearing on fire borrowing.

Happily for Louisiana we do not have forest fires like in the West because we're actually managing the Kisatchie Forest and doing prescribed burns and clearing the underbrush to prevent the fires and increasing our timber harvest. Interestingly the southeast forest which the forester, our Chief Forester testified, is really a model, potentially, for some of our brethren out in the West because we're seeing so much success.

Now we don't have the similar climate as the West. We don't have the drought conditions. But some of our pilots have been extremely successful. So I'm looking forward to sharing that.

But thank you.

But our time is running short, but Senator Lee—and I know this is very important. If you wanted to just have a question or two. We need to close up in about five or so minutes.

But go ahead.

Senator LEE. Thank you very much, Madame Chair.

Thanks to all of you for joining us.

Dr. Nelson, it's great to see you again. I was wondering if you could tell us just a little bit about what's happening in Utah. I know in Utah, like so many other places, production on Federal lands has been declining even while production overall has been on the increase.

Of course, what makes that so significant is that two-thirds of our land is Federal.

So how is Utah able to do that? What can you tell us about the sufficiency of the environmental restrictions that we have on the books in Utah? Is Utah able to achieve these things on the non Federal lands without degrading the environment?

Mr. NELSON. Thank you, Senator Lee. I really appreciate that question. It's also very nice to see you again as well.

Maybe I'll try to address that question and also maybe provide some concluding comments, Madame Chair.

I think local management of resource is really key. I think your example of forest management and prevention of fires is key. We work very closely with our local regulators, with our communities, with industry to manage all of our resources.

As I mentioned at the beginning of my testimony, we not only have these conventional energy resources which are so important to the vitality of our economy, we also have beautiful landscapes and vistas that we want to protect. We have a proven track record of restoration and collaborative efforts in Utah.

So I'll go back to, kind of, my point that really there are 2 key issues.

One is access to the resources and our ability to, in Utah, to effectively manage those resources.

So the challenge is on permitting with regard to federally managed lands are very, very difficult. They, as I mentioned with respect to solar developments, the process of getting a project done is just too lengthy to even realize the benefits of those very popular resources and supported resources today, not to mention for some of our conventional resources.

So we have targeted State lands and private lands recently to see increases, but we will continue to work with our communities, with policymakers, with local stakeholders, with regulators to balance both the environmental and the development outcomes.

Senator LEE. If I can ask one follow up.

So when we do have significant development going on elsewhere in the State, but we have diminished development on Federal lands, I think this ends up adversely, disproportionately affecting some parts of the State where the percentage of Federal land is even higher than the statewide average of two-thirds. We've got some counties where the Federal Government owns well in excess of 90 percent of the land.

Can you tell us a little bit about how that affects some of these communities at a local, real level when Federal production is diminished either as a result of an unnecessarily prolonged permitting process or otherwise?

Mr. NELSON. I think one of the things that we see in a lot of these rural communities, I mentioned energy jobs are particularly high paying. They're 190 percent of the average wage in Utah. When these communities can't develop those particular resources what we see is that there really is stagnation in their ability to realize higher incomes and also to realize higher levels of employment.

So what we see in these communities is typically that they are subject to lower wage jobs and they're also subject to longer periods of suppressed employment. So I think that access to those resources is critical for bringing up wages in our rural communities, in particular, because I think they are disproportionately impacted and also allowing them the same favorable opportunities for economic growth.

Senator LEE. Great.

Thank you, Dr. Nelson.

Thank you, Madame Chair.

The CHAIR. Thank you.

Mr. Shafer, your last word and then Mr. Taylor and we're going to adjourn.

Mr. SHAFER. I guess just a quick response to Senator Sanders. I think the thing that people should understand is that the U.S. and the world is going to continue to consume oil and gas for the foreseeable future. The real question is do we produce it here or do we produce it overseas?

If we produce it here that means jobs. That means government revenues. Really that means regulations in the U.S. safety, focus on safety, focus on the environment, compared to some of the other countries less developed, less strict regulatory requirements.

So it's not really a yes or no oil and gas at this point in time. It's a yes or no U.S. jobs, U.S. Government revenue.

The CHAIR. Thank you.

Mr. Taylor.

Mr. TAYLOR. Thank you.

I can also close with a Utah example. What's going on in Utah with Congressman Bishop and others is they've got all the counties, all the stakeholders together, trying to figure out the best way to manage public lands. They've essentially got everyone in a room talking to each other and hammering this stuff out.

That is the way forward in our belief. But through it accomplish all of our goals with these obvious, you know, butting of heads and what have you. So we would encourage, you know, that model to be followed and not the model of simply drawing an enormous circle around a big map and saying this is going to be specially designated. We're going to manage it to limit uses.

The CHAIR. I'd like to end with putting the lands map up, please, that we had. Say that, you know, this committee takes this work very, very seriously, broadly. There are very divergent views.

But as Chair I really want to forge a compromise on this use of resources for the Nation to create jobs, to expand prosperity, to help build a middle class, to be sensitive to the environment and very, very sensitive to the local community's ability to work these issues out to achieve all those ends. I don't think it has to be an either/or. I think we can find a way.

For the States that have high land under the Federal Government. The Federal Government is going to have to be more cooperative to achieve this. Because they are a big stakeholder, I mean, 81 percent of the land is owned by the Federal Government in Nevada. So achieving this cannot be achieved without the Federal partners leaning forward.

Now in Louisiana only 4.6 percent of our land is federally owned. We can do a lot of things. If we could just get revenue sharing we could save our coast. We're going to have to and we need a partner to do that.

In some of the other States it's minimus the amount of—diminimus the amount of money that—the amount of land that is owned by the Federal Government. So this is like, Senator Lee, when I put this graph up it really shows us, you know, how the West has such a different.

You can understand view of this then the East Coast States, but this is one Congress for all States. So we're going to have to find a way forward which is not going to be easy, but definitely doable, and accomplish some great things over the next year or 2 or 3 or more.

So, thank you all very much.

Meeting adjourned.

[Whereupon, at 1:01 p.m. the hearing was adjourned.]

# APPENDIXES

## APPENDIX I

### Responses to Additional Questions

RESPONSES OF SEAN SHAFER TO QUESTIONS FROM SENATOR LANDRIEU

*Question 1.* In your testimony, you state that the federal government alone receives $85 million per day from the oil and natural gas industry while state and local governments receive millions more. According to experts with the American Petroleum Institute, this $85 million is a combination of two income streams that includes: (1) rents, royalties and bonuses from production or access to development on federal lands; and (2) corporate income taxes paid by refiners and exploration and production businesses and reflected in IRS reporting data. In addition, your testimony notes that offshore production is estimated to provide more than $9 billion/per year to the federal government.

A. Can you explain how this $85 million—or, generally, how much of this revenue is contributed by offshore production? Onshore production?

Answer. Approximately $25 million of this daily revenue is associated with offshore production, with the remainder attributable to onshore production. Government revenues from offshore production are higher relative to production than onhsore production as almost all offshore production in the U.S. takes places in federal waters in comparison to onshore production which takes place primarily on private land. This is because of the federal government receives all royalties (and shares them to a limited extent with certain states) for federal offshore production offshore production, whereas royalties from onshore production on private land are collected by private land owners.

*Question 2.* In your testimony, you assert that Quest Offshore has determined that the offshore oil and gas industry has produced 375,000 jobs, but that the contributions of the offshore oil and gas industry are limited due to the fact that approximately 85 percent of acreage of federal offshore waters is inaccessible to development. You go on to point out that Atlantic Coast OCS activities, if allowed, could create an additional 80,000 jobs and would generate an addition $645 million per year in additional federal revenue by 2025.

A. Can you explain what percentage of the current 85 percent of inaccessible acreage includes the Atlantic OCS in your projections? Sean Shafer: The Atlantic OCs is approximately 15.7 percent of the total OCS which corresponds to approximately 19 percent of the areas unavailable to offshore oil and gas production.

B. More broadly, has Quest Offshore prepared estimates on how much revenue and jobs could be generated if offshore development were to be expanded to federal offshore waters in addition to the Atlantic OCS?

Answer. Total government revenues from Atlantic OCS oil and gas activity were projected to reach over $12.1 billion, with the split between federal and state revenues dependent on new legislation. Quest is currently completing analysis on the Pacific OCS and the areas of the Eastern Gulf of Mexico which are currently inaccessible. From this analysis opening the Pacific OCS to new oil and gas activity could lead to the creation of around 330 thousand jobs and $15.7 billion of new government revenue by 2035. Opening the areas of the Eastern Gulf of Mexico currently inaccessible to oil and gas activity could lead to the creation of around 230 thousand jobs and $10.4 billion of government revenue by 2035.

RESPONSE OF SEAN SHAFER TO QUESTION FROM SENATOR SCOTT

*Question 1.* Recently, BOEM released an updated assessment of the oil and natural gas resources in the Atlantic OCS that showed a 43 percent increase in oil and a 20 percent increase in natural gas. How would this increase in resource estimates impact the numbers in your Atlantic OCS study?

Answer. The study anticipated increasing resource estimates in the Atlantic OCS due to historical trends in resource estimates in areas such as the Gulf of Mexico and North Sea as areas are explored. However, the increased resource estimates likely make the study more conservative and indicate additional upside for oil production in the Atlantic OCS. This increased upside in oil production would be expected to correlate with an increased upside in job creation, government revenues, GDP and other effects of Atlantic OCS oil and natural gas production.

———

RESPONSE OF JOEL WEBSTER TO QUESTION FROM SENATOR LANDRIEU

*Question 1.* In your testimony, you mentioned proposals to provide public access to currently landlocked public lands, which I support. Can you elaborate?

Answer. The number one reason hunters and anglers stop pursuing their outdoor pastimes is lack of access. It begins with a single bad experience in the outdoors, perhaps an unexpectedly locked gate, an overly-crowded boat ramp, a no trespassing sign; then this problem of reduced access and diminished quality of experience metastasizes over a hunting season or two, until sportsmen -and women ultimately decide not to purchase licenses, permits, tags, ammunition, hunting gear, fuel, food, and lodging. The negative economic impacts that occur when people stop hunting and fishing are profound, and impact communities across the country, and certainly in Louisiana, in a way that means fewer jobs and less money for conservation.

Answer. The first major proposal to enhance public access is the Land and Water Conservation Fund. LWCF has only been fully funded twice in its 50 year history, and yet still the program has produced meaningful benefits for American sportsmen. There are examples across the country of LWCF dollars that have expanded access for hunters and anglers, making tracts large and small available for outdoor recreationists, and improving wildlife habitat. Each year, as Louisiana's resident and non-resident waterfowl hunters head to the marsh, they could well have in their sights mallards and pintails that hatched in wetlands protected with LWCF dollars. The funding mechanism for LWCF expires soon, and Congress will likely be debating an LWCF reauthorization package; LWCF should not only be reauthorized, but it should also be taken off-budget and treated as a true trust fund, and not to be subject to the annual appropriations process.

The second proposal for enhancing sportsmen's access that TRCP supports is the Making Public Lands Public initiative, which would utilize 1.5 percent of LWCF funds for use in projects specifically aimed at enhancing recreation access. For the past several years, President Obama has included MPLP in his budget request, and much has been done administratively via this provision to improve access. TRCP and nearly the entirety of the sportsmen's community believes it is imperative that the Making Public Lands Public concept be memorialized in statute, as was attempted in the recent floor consideration of the Bipartisan Sportsmen's Act of 2014. Making Public Lands Public also underscores the need for durable off-budget reauthorization of the underlying LWCF program.

The third legislative vehicle for improving sportsmen's access is the Hunt Unrestricted on National Treasures (HUNT) Act. Similar to the Making Public Lands Public concept, the HUNT Act specifically targets public lands made inaccessible by prevailing land ownership patterns. The HUNT Act would require BLM and the USFS to determine where large tracts of "landlocked" public lands exist, and then identify the steps necessary to make those lands accessible to the public. A recent report indicates that as many as 4 million landlocked acres may exist across the West. After identifying both the tracts, and the barriers to access, the HUNT Act would utilize 1.5 percent of LWCF dollars to purchase voluntary access easements from willing landowners to open these public lands to use by their owners, the public. In some cases, a small investment in a spur trail or parking lot, could open tens of thousands of acres to public use, a wise investment in the future of hunting and angling.

These three interrelated programs comprise a significant portion of the sporting community's access initiative. Of course, there are many programs, from the Forest Service Legacy Roads Program, to the Fish and Wildlife Fish Passage Program, to the USDA's Voluntary Public Access program that improve not just access, but improve the quality of the habitat that's being accessed. Because it's not just about having open gates, but what is on the other side of those open gates, that matters. We sincerely thank you for the opportunity to testify, and to provide you with this further information on access, one of the most important issues to America's hunters and anglers today.

RESPONSES OF LAURA NELSON TO QUESTIONS FROM SENATOR LANDRIEU

*Question 1.* Do you think that all states that play host to energy production, whether onshore or offshore, should receive a fair share of those revenues back to the state or local communities that host that production? Why or why not?

Answer. Yes, we absolutely believe that states should received their fair share of mineral lease royalties, and that comparable percentages should be contemplated regardless of a facility's onshore or offshore status.

With respect to western states in particular, given the unusually large portion of federal lands in the states located to the north, south, and west of Colorado (28-81%), the 50% royalty allocation is simply not enough to mediate development impacts and support our educational systems and other needs. 50% may suffice for a prospective offshore wind state such as Massachusetts, because only 1.6% of the land in that state is federally owned. This matters because a state like Massachusetts—or Pennsylvania, and other Eastern states—has enough of a tax base to support its social needs. Conversely, in a state with approximately 70% of its land under federal control, if federal mineral lease royalties and other associated revenues are not fairly allocated, communities will undoubtedly be underserved. Impacts extend beyond the communities where development takes place and royalty allocation needs to meet the peripheral impacts, as well.

A more sensible approach would be to allocate royalties to states on a sliding scale associated with the portion of the state under federal control. Such an arrangement would not mean one deal for Alaska (~90%) and one deal for "everyone else" (~50%), but rather a scenario in which Utah and Nevada were treated in a way that, appropriately, was more comparable to Alaska than, say, to Virginia. This would better ensure the efficient allocation of benefits and costs of developing resources that contribute to our regional and national welfare.

*Question 2.* In your testimony, you mentioned that "Utah's goal is to take back the reins" on resource development. I understand that almost 70% of Utah's lands are owned by the Federal Government. How do you balance your desire for more Utah state control over resources when the Federal Government owns such a large majority of the land?

Answer. There are a variety of ways. One of the primary paths forward, as suggested by Rep. Bishop's good work in recent years, is to pursue comprehensive land swaps that help consolidate lands of priority for federal land management agencies while doing the same for the state. While this may do little to affect the simple percentage of land in federal hands, it can have a dramatic effect on the state's ability to access its resources. This is true because it allows the state to take its dispersed checkerboard of holdings and consolidate them in areas of high economic value. Not only does this improve access to specific, concentrated resources, but it also adds value because the larger the area, the less likely that a costly federal nexus will be established by the construction of an access road, a transmission facility, etc. Land swaps are an important opportunity that require our ongoing commitment and diligence.

Another opportunity is in further delegation of regulatory responsibilities for activities underway on public lands. Our experience has been that federal regulation in the realm of energy development is steered equally by science and by controversy. This unfortunate approach leads to over-zealous regulation that is not reasonable from a cost-benefit perspective, and that puts an undue burden on companies hoping to invest and create jobs in our rural communities. States like Utah, on the other hand, tend to base their regulations on a sensible "best practices" approach that leads to comparable outcomes at far less expense. The federal government should recognize states with good regulatory track records, judging by environmental outcomes not environmentalist outcries, and should be prepared to delegate regulatory authority accordingly.

*Question 3.* As a follow up, in your testimony, you call for the Federal Government to support an increased role for Utah in managing its resources. Can you give me some examples of concrete steps that could be taken to achieve this?

Answer. Utah has demonstrated its ability and willingness to manage its resources in a number of ways, including, but not limited to, preserving threatened species, regulating hydraulic fracturing practices, and pursuing land exchanges that advance multiple goals.

Utah's Grahams Penstemon Conservation Agreement is a recent example of diverse stakeholders working together within the state to chart a species management path free of cumbersome Federal regulations. Agreement stakeholders included industry, state and local officials, tribal representatives, and the U.S. Fish and Wildlife Service (FWS), who came together to develop an approach that would advance both conservation and development goals. Utah believes a similar approach can be successful in addressing the sage grouse and other species of concern. Currently, Utah's plan for sage grouse, which was developed through a comprehensive stakeholder process, would result in protection of over 90% of sage grouse population in the state. Impediments to implementation of such compromise-driven initiatives have come from special interests whose aim is to discourage development generally. Utah believes that substantial progress in managing the sage grouse and other species can best be accomplished by deferring to state-based plans that address the concerns of the FWS, and that benefit from local knowledge and expertise in the protection of sensitive species populations.

In addition to species management, Utah has a significant regulatory track record in managing the development of its resources. A key example of Utah's regulatory competency is in the area of hydraulic fracturing, a technique that has been employed in Utah for decades without a single recorded incident of water contamination or other adverse consequences. Another example is the process—and timeline—by which the state reviews and approves applications for permits to drill (APD). Utah believes that its effective approach to both the regulation of well stimulation techniques and disclosure, and its streamlined approach to managing APDs, are just two examples of how efficient state processes often are by comparison to their federal counterparts. Federal land management agencies should be encouraged either to delegate regulatory authority to the states, or alternatively to adopt state-specific regulatory approaches that have proven timely and productive for state regulators.

Collaborative, compromise-oriented approaches to species management and streamlined regulatory practices established in partnership with states will be essential tools as we strive to make our public lands more productive. However, improving the management of public lands is just one way to increase states' roles in managing their resources. Another approach is simply through land swaps aimed at the equal advancement of development and conservation goals. Utah and its School and Institutional Trust Lands Administration (SITLA) have been leaders in identifying land exchanges that result in moving lands with conservation characteristics under Federal management and bringing resource development areas under state control. The benefits of land exchanges are significant and include better conservation, more efficient land development, and overall improved improved social, economic and environmental outcomes. The challenge is that timeframes for final approval of land exchanges have become increasingly lengthy, resulting in lost opportunities for both development and conservation. Utah encourages Congress to establish a streamlined process for approving land exchanges, one with definitive timelines aimed at eliminating the overwhelming process costs—and opportunity costs—that exist today.

# APPENDIX II

## Additional Material Submitted for the Record

---

NATIONAL CONFERENCE OF STATE HISTORIC PRESERVATION OFFICERS,
*444 North Capitol St., NW, Washington, DC., July 30, 2014*

Hon. MARY L. LANDRIEU,
*Chairman, Senate Committee on Energy and Natural Resources, 304 Dirksen Senate Office Building, Washington DC.*

Hon. LISA MURKOWSKI,
*Ranking Member, Senate Committee on Energy and Natural Resources, 709 Hart Senate, Office Building, Washington DC.*

DEAR CHAIRMAN LANDRIEU AND RANKING MEMBER MURKOWSKI:

On behalf of the members of the National Conference of State Historic Preservation Officers (NCSHPO) I write to share with you background and information on the Historic Preservation Fund (HPF) and how it's integrally related to your recent hearing titled "Leveraging America's Natural Resources as a Revenue Generator and Job Creator."

The NCSHPO is the professional association of the State government officials (State Historic Preservation Officers or SHPOs) who carry out the national historic preservation program as delegates of the Secretary of the Interior pursuant to the National Historic Preservation Act of 1966, as amended (NHPA) (16 USC 470). In 2013, SHPOs reviewed nearly 103,000 federal undertakings, delivered 82,100 national register eligibility opinions, provided guidance and technical assistance on nearly 1,200 historic tax credit projects, surveyed approximately 16.3 million acres and evaluated over 135,000 properties for their historical significance.

*HPF—History*

In 1976 the National Historic Preservation Act was amended to create a funding stream, called the Historic Preservation Fund (HPF), to implement the national historic preservation program as an efficient federal/state partnership on behalf of the Department of Interior. The HPF provides matching funds to SHPOs and grants to Tribal Historic Preservation Offices who carry out the preservation programs that preserve and utilize our nation's historic resources and simultaneously generate revenue and jobs. Currently, $150 million is deposited annually into the HPF. However, recent appropriations have languished at about one-third of the authorized amount. The current authorization expires September 30, 2015.

Like the Land and Water Conservation Fund, HPF income is derived from offshore oil lease revenues. Following the same principal, a portion of these Outer Continental Shelf (OCS) revenues, derived from the depletion of non-renewable resources, results in the preservation of another non-renewable resource—our Nation's historic places which serve as a permanent legacy to all Americans.

*HPF—Jobs and Economic Development*

   *Community Revitalization*

Nationwide, communities have experienced how historic preservation plays a prominent and effective role in community and neighborhood revitalization. Historic preservation combats the effects of blight and disinvestment by using the historic built environment as a catalyst for community change. These changes result in thriving historic downtown districts, Main Streets, and neighborhoods becoming "destinations" consisting of restaurants, office space, art galleries, specialty shops, living spaces, and civic centers.

Historic Main Streets are also frequently the heart and soul of a community. It is not, the nondescript shopping centers or malls which people rally around saving, tour on vacations, or use as the enduring descriptive "center" of their home towns. According to the National Main Street Center, in 2013, local Main Street programs throughout the country experienced a net gain in businesses and jobs of 115,381 and 502,278, respectively. The total number of building rehabilitations was 246,158 and the total reinvestment in physical improvements was nearly $60 billion. In 2013 in Louisiana, 194 new Main Street businesses opened creating 527 new jobs and new rehabilitation and construction projects totaled $14 million.

Historic preservation programs, such as in Juneau and Skagway, serve not only as a means of preserving a community's history, but they provide a vehicle for guiding that community's growth in the future—spurring economic development and tourism while trying to save what makes those places distinctive. For the past ten years, the Alaska Department of Transportation has promoted the scenic byways program and enhanced visitor attractions, including several historic buildings, along Alaska's highways. The agency has also installed interpretive signs at a number of highway waysides.

### Historic Tax Credit

The Federal Rehabilitation Tax Credit (HTC) program, administered primarily by the State Historic Preservation Offices with funding from the Historic Preservation Fund, is an important driver in economic development. The program benefits communities by:

- Increasing the value of the rehabilitated property by returning vacant or underutilized structures to the tax roles and stimulating adjacent development projects.
- Encouraging protection of landmarks through the promotion, recognition, and designation of historic structures, and acting as a catalyst for further community renewal.
- Revitalizing downtowns and neighborhoods and, since sometimes paired with the Low Income Housing Tax Credit, at times increasing the amount of available housing within the community.

Since inception, the HTC has rehabilitated nearly 39,000 buildings, created 2.4 million jobs and leveraged $109 billion in private investment nationwide. On average, the HTC leverages $5 dollars in private investment for every $1 dollar in federal funding creating highly effective public-private partnerships. In 2013, the HTC spurred $3.39 billion in rehabilitation work, created nearly 63,000 skilled, local jobs and over 25,000 new or renovated housing units. All of which brings short and long-term economic opportunities for the community.

In 2013, the HTC leveraged over $239 million in private investment in Louisiana's historic, income-producing buildings. The Louisiana State Commercial & Residential Tax Credit Programs leveraged over $128 million in private investment in Louisiana's historic buildings and both programs created a total of 3,871 construction jobs.

### Heritage Tourism

Heritage tourism also creates jobs, new businesses, builds community pride and can improve quality of life. Funding for SHPOs through the HPF provides the essential resources needed to partner with communities in identifying historic places and providing research for tourism interpretation and materials. According to a 2009 national research study on U.S. Cultural and Heritage Travel by Mandela Research, 78% of all U.S. leisure travelers participate in cultural and/or heritage activities while traveling translating to 118.3 million adults each year. Cultural and heritage visitors spend, on average, $994 per trip compared to $611 for all U.S. travelers. Perhaps the biggest benefits of cultural heritage tourism, though, are diversification of local economies and preservation of a community's unique character.

Alaska's tourism industry is a key economic driver for the State. In 2013 the out-of-state visitors totaled nearly 2 million and is anticipated to continue increasing. When surveyed, many visitors said they enjoyed heritage sites and learning how people lived in the north. The totem parks at Ketchikan and Saxman, the gold rush era town of Skagway, the Alaska Native Heritage Center and Anchorage Museum at Rasmuson Center in Anchorage and the University of Alaska's Museum of the North in Fairbanks were among the top visitor destinations.

Tourism also plays a significant role in Louisiana. In 2013, 27.3 million visitors to Louisiana spent $10.8 billion, and contributed $800 million in state tax revenues. Many of these visitors came specifically to see and experience Louisiana's historic cultural and heritage sites. To date, Louisiana has 1,240 individual properties and 105 historic districts for a total of over 50,000 resources listed in the National Register of Historic Places as well as 53 National Historic Landmarks. In June, the Poverty Point State Historic Site also became the 1,001st property listed as World Heritage Site list which will generate additional tourism revenue from visitors around the world.

*HPF—Investing in America's Future*

By responsibly leveraging America's natural resources, by using a small fraction of Outer Continental Shelf revenues for the HPF, for almost 40 years historic preservation has generated billions of dollars in revenue at the local, state and federal levels, preserved our nation's diverse and significant historic resources, revitalized communities, and created millions of jobs.

As something that truly impacts the daily lives of so many Americans, this return on investment must continue. It is vital that the Senate Energy and Natural Resources Committee and all of Congress commit to reinvesting in our nation's historic resources through supporting permanent and full funding for the HPF—for the benefit of preserving the important historic resources of our past as well as for the future and for the economic well-being of our nation.

Sincerely,

ERIK HEIN,
*Executive Director.*

———

NATIONAL TRUST FOR HISTORIC PRESERVATION,
*August 5, 2014.*

Hon. MARY LANDRIEU,
*Chairman, Committee on Energy and Natural Resources, 304 Dirksen Senate Office Building, Washington, DC.*
Hon. LISA MURKOWSKI,
*Ranking Member, Committee on Energy and Natural Resources, 709 Hart Senate Office Building, Washington, DC.*
Re: "Leveraging America's Natural Resources as a Revenue Generator and Job Creator"

DEAR CHAIRMAN LANDRIEU AND RANKING MEMBER MURKOWSKI:

Thank you for holding your July 22 hearing on "Leveraging America's Natural Resources as a Revenue Generator and Job Creator." You and your witnesses described well the long legacy of allocating a portion of the revenues from the nation's natural resources, including the Outer Continental Shelf (OCS), to support important programs benefiting the American public.

The National Trust for Historic Preservation is a privately-funded nonprofit organization chartered by Congress in 1949. We work to save America's historic places to enrich our future. With headquarters in Washington, D.C., 13 field offices, 27 historic sites, 746,000 members and supporters and partner organizations in 50 states, territories, and the District of Columbia, the National Trust works to save America's historic places and advocates for historic preservation as a fundamental value in programs and policies at all levels of government.

Your hearing appropriately identified important legislative precedents for allocating portions of revenues from the use of federal natural resources to vitally important programs, including the Gulf of Mexico Energy Security Act (GOMESA), the RESTORE Act, Secure Rural Schools legislation, Payments in Lieu of Taxes (PILT) and the Land and Water Conservation Fund (LWCF), in addition to strongly supported but unsuccessful legislation such as the Conservation and Reinvestment Act (CARA) in 1999-2000 and the CLEAR Act of 2009-2010.

The National Trust believes strongly that any future legislation allocating OCS revenues should build upon the precedents of CARA and the CLEAR Act and also provide full and permanent funding for the Historic Preservation Fund (HPF). The HPF was created in 1976 to fund the nation's historic preservation programs. The HPF provides formula-based matching funds, administered by the National Park Service, to the State Historic Preservation Officers (SHPOs) and grants to Tribal Historic Preservation Officers (THPOs). These funds support the implementation of the nation's preservation programs, including Historic Tax Credit (HTC) applications, section 106 reviews, nominations for the National Register of Historic Places and surveys of historic resources. These activities are essential to protecting historic resources while also permitting the utilization of resources that generate revenues and jobs. For example, the HTC, signed into law by President Reagan, has catalyzed the rehabilitation of more than 39,600 buildings throughout the nation. Since its creation more than 30 years ago, the HTC has created 2.4 million jobs and leveraged nearly $109 billion in private investment.

Each year, the HPF receives $150 million from revenues generated from oil and gas development on the OCS. Similarly, the LWCF receives $900 million annually in OCS revenues. However, both funds are presently subject to annual appropriations, which vary from year to year. Since FY11, appropriations for the HPF have ranged between $53 million and $56.4 million. The FY14 Omnibus Appropriations bill also provided $500,000 to launch an important new program of competitive grants for the survey and nomination of properties associated with communities currently underrepresented in the National Register of Historic Places and National Historic Landmarks. Recent studies have documented that less than 8 percent of such listings identify culturally diverse properties.

In past years, the HPF also provided funding for the Save America's Treasures and Preserve America grant programs, as well as grants for Historically Black Colleges and Universities.

Full funding for the HPF would enable more robust funding for a broad range of preservation programs, including a restoration of competitive grants to restore nationally significant historic properties, similar to the Save America's Treasures program. It would also provide funding to meet the continuing demands upon SHPOs and THPOs for their preservation services, including the survey of historic resources. The funding pressures on THPOs continues to grow, in part because of the challenges of an increasing number of THPOs participating in the program, from 131 tribes in FY12 to potentially 156 tribes in FY15, with nearly level funding. Finally, another important preservation funding need—the digitization of legacy historic survey data, as called for by a $6 million request for grants to SHPO's and THPO's in the Administration's FY15 "Opportunity, Growth and Security Initiative," would improve access to historic property records and help expedite federal permitting of important infrastructure projects.

We look forward to working with you and the Committee as it addresses the challenges and significant opportunities to address the allocation of natural resource revenues for important national priorities, including full and permanent funding for the Historic Preservation Fund.

Sincerely,

THOMAS J. CASSIDY, JR.,
*Vice President for Government Relations and Policy.*

○